STANLEY MORISON

A PORTRAIT

THE TRUSTEES OF THE
BRITISH MUSEUM
LONDON
1971

ISBN 0 7141 0329 2
© The Trustees of the British Museum
1971

The catalogue of an exhibition held in the
King's Library, British Museum
8 July–3 October 1971

The monogram design on the cover and
title-page is by Reynolds Stone
Printed in Monotype Ehrhardt

Printed in Great Britain
at the University Printing House, Cambridge
(Brooke Crutchley, University Printer)

PREFACE

This exhibition pays tribute to one of the most influential – though surprisingly little known – Englishmen of his generation: Stanley Morison's was a many-sided personality, but his most important contribution was to the appearance of the printed page. The exhibition has therefore been timed to coincide with IPEX, the Twelfth International Printing Machinery and Allied Trades Exhibition being held at Earls Court and Olympia, and with the London meeting of the Association Typographique Internationale in July 1971.

It has been prepared with the assistance of an advisory committee consisting of a number of Morison's friends and colleagues: Messrs Nicolas Barker, John Carter, Brooke Crutchley, John Dreyfus and Graham Pollard. Mr Howard Nixon of this Department has acted as chairman of the committee. Mr John Barr has been responsible for the arrangement of the exhibits and for compiling the catalogue. The exhibition has been designed by the Museum's Exhibitions Office.

The Trustees of the British Museum wish to express their deep appreciation to the members of the committee for the help they have given in planning the exhibition and checking the catalogue entries, and for the loans they have made; as also to the other private lenders and to the firms and institutions whose loans have supplemented the Museum's resources. The Trustees would like in particular to thank Mr Nicolas Barker for making available the draft of his biography of Morison which has been extensively drawn on for this catalogue. They also gratefully acknowledge the information and advice provided by Mr Victor Clark, Mr James Dearden, Mr Allen Hutt, Mr James Moran, Mrs Esther Potter, Mr James Wells and by Mr Harry Carter who checked the draft of the catalogue. They would also like to thank the Greater London Council for the loan of photographs of buildings associated with Morison, which are not listed in the catalogue.

K. B. GARDNER
Principal Keeper of Printed Books

LIST OF LENDERS AND DONORS

A. V. Austin
Nicolas Barker
Lord Bridges
John Carter
Douglas Cleverdon
Revd J. H. Crehan, S.J.
Arthur Crook
John Dreyfus
Arie J. Gelderblom
Ben Grauer
Ronald Mansbridge
Dr Giovanni Mardersteig
Sir Francis Meynell
Graham Pollard
Hans Schmoller
Mrs Timothy Simon
Janet Stone
Denis Tegetmeier
Berthold Wolpe

The estate of the late Stanley Morison

Beaverbrook Library
Bibliothèque Royale, Brussels
The Curators of the Bodleian Library
British Broadcasting Corporation
The Committee of the Garrick Club
Greater London Council
London Transport
The Monotype Corporation
National Art Library, Victoria and Albert Museum
St Bride Printing Library
The Post Office
The Printer to the University, Oxford
Times Newspapers Ltd
The University Printing House, Cambridge
The Administrator of Westminster Cathedral

CONTENTS

NOTE

Unless other sources are cited, passages in the text of the catalogue in inverted commas are quotations from Morison, often his own annotations contained in the *Handlists*, where he refers to himself in the third person as 'S.M.'; or in nos. 57–82, from *A tally of types*.

The catalogue illustrations are reproduced by permission of the lenders of the exhibits and of the British Federation of Master Printers, the Cambridge University Printing House, the Grolier Club, the Monotype Corporation, Victor Gollancz Ltd, and Times Newspapers Ltd.

REFERENCES

Nicolas Barker: *The printer and the poet. An account of the printing of 'The Tapestry'.* Cambridge, privately printed, 1970.

John Carter: *A handlist of the writings of Stanley Morison.* Cambridge, privately printed, 1950.

— [Supplement]. P. M. Handover: 'Stanley Morison: a second handlist, 1950–59', in *Motif* 3.

Brooke Crutchley: *Two men. Walter Lewis and Stanley Morison at Cambridge.* Cambridge, privately printed, 1968.

John Dreyfus: 'Mr Morison as typographer', in *Signature* 3 (New series), March 1947, pp. 3–24.

John Dreyfus: 'The impact of Stanley Morison', in *The Penrose Annual*, 1969, pp. 94–111.

James Moran: 'Stanley Morison, 1889–1967': *The Monotype Recorder*, Autumn 1968.

Stanley Morison: *A tally of types cut for machine composition and introduced at the University Press, Cambridge, 1922–32.* Cambridge, privately printed, 1953.

Oliver Simon: *Printer and playground.* Faber & Faber: London, 1956.

*

Permission for quotation is gratefully acknowledged

EARLY YEARS: APPRENTICESHIP

Stanley Arthur Morison was born in Wanstead, Essex, on 6 May 1889, the only son of Arthur Andrew Morison, an improvident and unsuccessful commercial traveller, and of Alice Louisa Morison, née Cole. In 1893 the Morison family moved to London, and from about 1899 on were living in Harringay. Morison attended Owen's School near the Angel, Islington, a grammar school with strong City connexions, which he left in 1903, probably because his earnings were needed to supplement the family's income. After her husband left her, while Morison was still at school, the burden of caring for her son and two daughters fell on Morison's mother, a courageous and independent woman. She took work in a tobacconist's shop in Holloway, and Morison worked first as an office boy at six shillings a week, and from 1905 as a clerk in the London City Mission. In 1912 he took up an uncongenial post in the London branch of a French bank, from which he soon resigned to join the staff of a new printing journal, *The Imprint*.

Morison's mother was unusually intelligent, and well read in the works of Thomas Paine and other freethinking writers; to her, no doubt, he owed his early acquaintance with books and intellectual pursuits. He certainly inherited her strong character, rational outlook and egalitarian habit of mind. Although he later held, to some extent at least, her political opinions, he did not share her agnosticism. Possibly through reading the writings of Fr Herbert Thurston, S.J., the well-known and prolific Catholic apologist, Morison came to frequent the Jesuits at Farm Street; he became a friend of Thurston's and in December 1908 was received into the Roman Catholic Church.

Apart from his religion and his wide reading, three youthful enthusiasms stayed with Morison for many years: railways – especially the Great Northern Line – philately and cricket.

Morison's interest in printing led him to buy and read *The Times* Printing Number of 10 September 1912 [3] in which appeared an advertisement for the first number of *The Imprint*, a journal founded with the aim of raising the standard of commercial printing. In this first issue there was advertised a position on the staff of *The Imprint*, which Morison applied for and obtained.

Morison's achievements cannot be fully understood without some reference to the technical and aesthetic level of printing and type design in England before the First World War. Text was often set in debased and unattractive versions of 'Modern face', which mediocre press-work did little to enhance. With few exceptions, the printing trade in general paid little attention to type design; some 'Old faces' had from about 1840 on been reintroduced, but were considered suitable only for books with a 'period' flavour, and for devotional and liturgical books. William Morris had, however, both by precept and example led a renaissance of printing as a craft, with the result that the private press movement was producing well-made and beautiful books, although for a necessarily restricted public. These books were usually printed in types inspired by those of fifteenth-century Venice, especially those used by Nicolas Jenson.

In the composing rooms of commercial printers the setting of type by hand had gradually been superseded by mechanical setting on Linotype and Monotype machines, but the earliest founts of type designed for mechanical composition were merely copies of the 'Modern face', 'Old face', Clarendons and grotesques currently supplied by typefounders. In Beatrice Warde's words, 'the trouble with printing as a whole was that it wasn't a whole; it was still cut up into three separate worlds, with the "art" people, the "business" people and the "technical" people each convinced that only their world really mattered'. Morison's work with the Monotype Corporation did much to bring the beauty and high standards of workmanship of the private press books to the industrial production of books and newspapers.

At this stage, too, we should note the revival by Edward Johnston of the art of calligraphy, which was to regain its influence on almost all forms of lettering, including type faces. William Morris, John Ruskin and others had studied and in some measure imitated medieval manuscripts. Edward Johnston's work, however, so impressed W. R. Lethaby, Principal of the Central School of Arts and Crafts, that Johnston was asked to teach practical lettering and illumination in classes which began in September 1899. Eric Gill was among the first seven students, and Adrian Fortescue, a newly ordained Catholic priest, soon joined – both later became friends of Morison's. Morison met Johnston in 1913 and was interested in Johnston's text-book, *Writing and illuminating and lettering*, 1906. Around 1916 he adopted the chancery italic hand, illustrated and commended in Johnston's book, for his own handwriting.

1. Morison's birth certificate 6 May 1889

2. Early photographs of Morison
   (*Lent by the estate of the late Stanley Morison*)
(a) A photograph taken July 1903.
(b) A photograph of Morison wearing pince-nez, inscribed on the back 'Stanley at Ostend'.
(c) A photograph taken about 1914.
(d) A photograph taken at Leigh-on-Sea, Essex.

3. 'The Times' Printing Number, 10 September 1912
On his way home from the City Morison bought at King's Cross Station a copy of *The Times* containing a Printing Supplement – the idea was Lord Northcliffe's. This supplement, which Morison considered a 'spectacular' production, enlightened him on most aspects of printing and its allied trades and encouraged him to study them further. It included articles on many of Morison's future interests: 'The origin and growth of the British newspaper', '*The Times*: its relation to the art of printing', 'The Monotype and Linotype machines', 'Postage stamps: how they are printed', 'Private printing presses'. Morison also saw the advertisement for a new periodical, *The Imprint*, not type-set but a reproduction of fine calligraphy – the unmistakable work of Edward Johnston. He bought the first issue.

4. 'The Imprint', no. 1, 13 January 1913, pp. vi–vii
The Imprint was founded by Gerard Meynell, owner of the Westminster Press, F. Ernest Jackson, J. H. Mason and Edward Johnston. Their purpose was to advocate improvement in the social and material conditions of work in the printing trade, to disseminate technical information and to raise printing to the standards, especially in type design, of the private presses. For the first issue a new type was cut by the Monotype Corporation to the specification of the editors, one of whom, Meynell, acted as intermediary with the Corporation. The new face called 'Imprint' was from the first available for sale to the trade without restriction, and its success proved to most people's satisfaction that mechanically set type could rival in appearance the best examples of composition by hand.

The note on the new 'Imprint' face is followed by the advertisement to which Morison replied. Although he had no experience in publishing or advertising, his enthusiasm for printing impressed Meynell and so he got the job.

5. (a) Morison's letter of application to the Director of the British Museum for a reader's ticket, 14 June 1913
(b) Morison's most recent reader's ticket

In a letter written from *The Imprint*, 11 Henrietta Street, Covent Garden, on 14 June 1913 Morison applied for a reader's ticket for the British Museum Reading Room in order to consult 'works dealing with liturgy and early printed service books'. Ticket no. B.3202 was issued to him on 25 June 1913 for six months, and later renewed. Morison's early acquaintance with A. W. Pollard, Keeper of Printed Books at the British Museum, is significant: Pollard directed Morison's attention to the sixteenth-century printers of Paris and Lyons, and to the modern printing of the Americans Bruce Rogers and D. B. Updike.

Before he was old enough to hold a reader's ticket Morison spent a great deal of his spare time in the Museum. It was there that as a boy, 'I first set eyes on the Rosetta Stone...and began to wonder why the several branches of the human family wrote in the funny ways they did...In the Grenville Library and the King's Library, and from the low-price guides that the Trustees publish, I found my attention turning to the form of books, manuscript and printed; to the art of writing and printing; and to the technicalities of production.'

6. 'Notes on some liturgical books' in 'The Imprint', no. 8, 27 August 1913, pp. (48)–60

Morison's earliest publication was the result of his study in the Reading Room of the British Museum. It was his interest in liturgical books which did much to introduce Morison to good printing. He formed his own collection of liturgical literature which, apart from those volumes destroyed by bombing, was later sold to the Newberry Library in Chicago.

BURNS & OATES

Towards the end of 1913 *The Imprint* was failing as a business venture, and Gerard Meynell introduced Morison to his uncle Wilfrid Meynell, managing director of the Catholic publishing firm of Burns & Oates and an amateur of good printing. Wilfrid had placed his youngest son Francis in charge of the firm's book design, and when Morison was invited to join the staff, nominally as a shorthand typist, he soon became Francis Meynell's assistant. Francis (later Sir Francis) Meynell was to found the Nonesuch Press in 1923 expressly to produce fine books by mechanical composition rather than hand-setting, and later became typographical adviser to H.M. Stationery Office.

The two young men produced a number of books, and at Burns & Oates Morison's circle of friends and range of typographical experience widened, to include Eric Gill, Fr Adrian Fortescue, Charles Jacobi, manager of the Chiswick Press, and Bernard Newdigate, whose Arden Press at Letchworth (where Fortescue was parish priest of St Hugh's) had printed for Burns & Oates since 1905. Newdigate later wrote the book-production notes in the *London Mercury*, commenting on many of the type faces introduced by Morison.

On 18 March 1916 Morison married Mabel Williamson; they later separated. There were no children of the marriage.

7. **Ordo administrandi sacramenta.**
   Londini apud Burns et Oates, 1915

This book is one of several designed by Morison
and Meynell which were printed in the Fell types
at the Oxford University Press.

8. **'Pange lingua.' Breviary hymns of old**
   Uses with an English rendering by Alan
   G. McDougall & an introduction by
   Adrian Fortescue. Burns & Oates:
   London, 1916

This book, printed by the Chiswick Press, is
another example of Morison's designs for Burns &
Oates.

9. **Letter from Morison to Wilfrid Mey-**
   nell, 24 June 1919
                              (*Lent by Sir Francis Meynell*)

Morison maintained his connexion with Burns &
Oates on a part-time basis.

10. **Envelope in the handwriting of Adrian**
    Fortescue (*Lent by Nicolas Barker Esq.*)

This envelope is addressed by Fr Adrian Fortescue in his distinctive hand to Morison. Fortescue wrote and designed for Burns & Oates
where Morison met him; he was an artist and
calligrapher of some skill and a well-known
liturgical scholar, author of books on the Eastern
Churches and of the standard work in English,
Ceremonies of the Roman Rite described. Of Fortescue's learning and personality Morison ab-
sorbed a great deal, and he even came to imitate
some of his mannerisms; to the end of his life
Morison wore black clothes and a hat like
Fortescue's [164].

11. **Boethius: 'De consolatione**
    philosophiae libri quinque'. (Edited by
    Adrian Fortescue.) Londinii: Burns,
    Oates & Washbourne Ltd., 1925.
    (Printed at the Cambridge University
    Press)
    — **Book jacket for this edition**
                              (*Lent by Graham Pollard Esq.*)

A cherished project of Adrian Fortescue's last
years was his posthumously published edition of
Boethius, and the book was designed for him with
great care and devotion by Morison. John Dreyfus
in 'Mr Morison as typographer' (*Signature*,
March 1947, p. 15) commends 'the sober ingenuity with which an annotated text, with com-
ments on the annotations, was presented for easy
reading'.

Morison's design for the jacket for this book
reproduces the layout of the title page.

12. **Alice Meynell: 'Ten poems, 1913–1915'.**
    Romney Street Press: Westminster,
    1915

On a printing press in Meynell's dining room
at 67 Romney Street, Westminster, Morison
helped Meynell to print two books, *The diary of
Mary Cary* and *Ten poems* by Meynell's mother.
The Oxford University Press provided Meynell
with two cases of the Fell type in the English size,
and this was probably the first time that Meynell
or Morison ever handled type themselves. The
colophon of *Ten poems* reads: 'Of these poems
fifty copies have been printed by Francis Meynell
and others in the Fell type, September 1915.
Rubricated by Edward Johnston, December
1915.'

13. **The Guild of the Pope's Peace: Preliminary notice.**
— **Prayer of Pope Benedict XV**
(Lent by Sir Francis Meynell)

On 27 January 1916 the Military Service (No. 2) Bill became law, which provided that all men between the ages of 18 and 41 who had been unmarried on 2 November 1915 should be deemed to have enlisted. Both Meynell and Morison were eligible for conscription, and both determined to refuse on conscientious grounds.

With a few of their fellow Catholics they set up a Catholic pacifist society, of which Meynell later said: 'Seldom, I think, can a propaganda body have had such handsome printing! It had little else!' A number of the Guild's leaflets were printed by the Pelican Press, founded by Meynell in 1916.

14. **Postcard from Morison to his mother, dated Aldershot, 9 July 1916**
(Lent by the estate of the late Stanley Morison)

Morison's appeal against conscription as a conscientious objector failed, and he was court-martialled for refusal to obey orders. He wrote to his mother: 'Today sentenced to two months hard labour for refusing to obey orders, to be served at H.M. Prison, Winchester, which will be my address for this "stretch". Hope all well. Will write again when able. Stan.'

For those conscientious objectors who refused to perform 'alternative employment of national importance', work centres were set up to provide occupations which would not conflict with their principles; the conditions were often disagreeable and unhealthy. Morison was sent to several of these centres, where he made friends with the Communists R. Palme Dutt, Robert Page Arnot and other political war resisters. After a brief discharge in 1917, possibly on grounds of sickness, he returned to the work centre in a disused prison at Wakefield.

15. **Programmes for performances in Wakefield Prison of G. B. Shaw's 'Fanny's first play' and 'Major Barbara', February and April 1918. (Printed by the Pelican Press)**
(Lent by A. V. Austin Esq.)

A light-hearted souvenir of a generally depressing period in Morison's life survives in these programmes for performances by the prisoners at Wakefield of *Fanny's first play* (the cast-list reads 'Major Knox: Stanley Morison') and *Major Barbara* ('Peter Shirley: Stanley Morison'). In April 1918, with the war coming to an end, Morison at last accepted 'alternative employment of national importance' and saw the war out working on a tomato farm at Finchley.

16. **Postcard from Morison to Fr Herbert Thurston, dated Hampstead, Trinity Sunday 1918**
(Lent by the Revd J. H. Crehan, S.J.)

Morison gives his views on certain Theosophical publications.

17. **'Some fruits of Theosophy. The origins and purposes of the so-called Old Catholic Church disclosed by Stanley Morison.' With a preface by Herbert Thurston, S.J.**
Harding and More: London, 1919

Morison's friend Fr Thurston (1856–1939), a noted Catholic polemicist and student of heterodox sects and 'fringe' religions, was the Jesuit who had instructed Morison in preparation for his baptism.

Perceiving Morison's depression after his period of detention as a conscientious objector, and his need of mental exercise and stimulus, Fr Thurston suggested and encouraged Morison's investigation into the claims of 'Archbishop' Arnold Mathew, a freelance ecclesiastic of doubtful antecedents. Morison's first published book is an exploration of the clerical underworld, and not an attack on the Theosophical Society as such (some of whose members had, after all, put up the money for the Pelican Press) nor on the Old Catholic Church which separated from the Roman Catholic Church after the declaration of the dogma of Papal Infallibility.

THE PELICAN PRESS

In 1916 Francis Meynell left his father's firm, Burns & Oates, to become business manager of the Socialist paper, the *Herald*, then appearing as a weekly. With the backing of two Theosophist ladies a printing office was also set up to exploit Meynell's typographical skill in the interests of both Socialism and Theosophy. Thus the Pelican Press was opened at 2 Gough Square in the early summer of 1916; run by Meynell it was in effect a branch of the Victoria House Printing Co., printers of the *Herald*. With Monotype machines and imported display faces the Pelican Press offered a great choice of type faces, and soon attracted a wide range of customers.

In March 1919 when the *Herald* became the *Daily Herald* again, Meynell, now assistant editor, was fully occupied and asked Morison to take his place at the Pelican Press as 'designer of printed matter'. Morison's and Meynell's design was often sixteenth-century French in style.

The variety of work and of customers rapidly broadened Morison's experience, but in September 1920 Meynell was obliged for political considerations to resign from the *Herald*. He returned to his former position at the Pelican Press, and Morison began to look for another job.

18. 'The types, borders, ornaments, initial letters, flowers and decorations of the Pelican Press set out for the satisfaction and convenience of customers and published Anno Domini 1921'
— Envelope

(*Lent by the Curators of the Bodleian Library*)
To mark the Pelican Press's acquisition of Cochin types from Peignot, the Paris typefounders, Morison designed a broadsheet specimen in black and red (together with an envelope) showing not only the range of type faces available but also an 'unrivalled' collection of printers' flowers, initials, 'factotums' and decorative borders. He described it in *The craft of printing*, 1921 [20], p. 12: 'The sheet consists of a magnificent piece of printing in red and black, size quad crown (40 inches by 30 inches). On one side is displayed full ranges of the Caslon, Cloister, Kennerley and Forum types (these last three newly marketed by the American Type Founders Company), also the remarkably fine and complete series (not to be found elsewhere in this country) of the 18th century types, namely, the Cochin, the Nicolas Cochin, the Moreau-le-Jeune, and the Fournier-le-Jeune. A choice of sumptuous borders, re-cut on wood...after Ratdolt, Tory and Jean de Tournes models, and a series of decorative initials and printers' flowers, completes the *verso* of the sheet.'

19. Bede Jarrett: 'Living temples'.
Burns & Oates: London, 1919
This book bears Morison's name in the colophon – a rare occurrence.

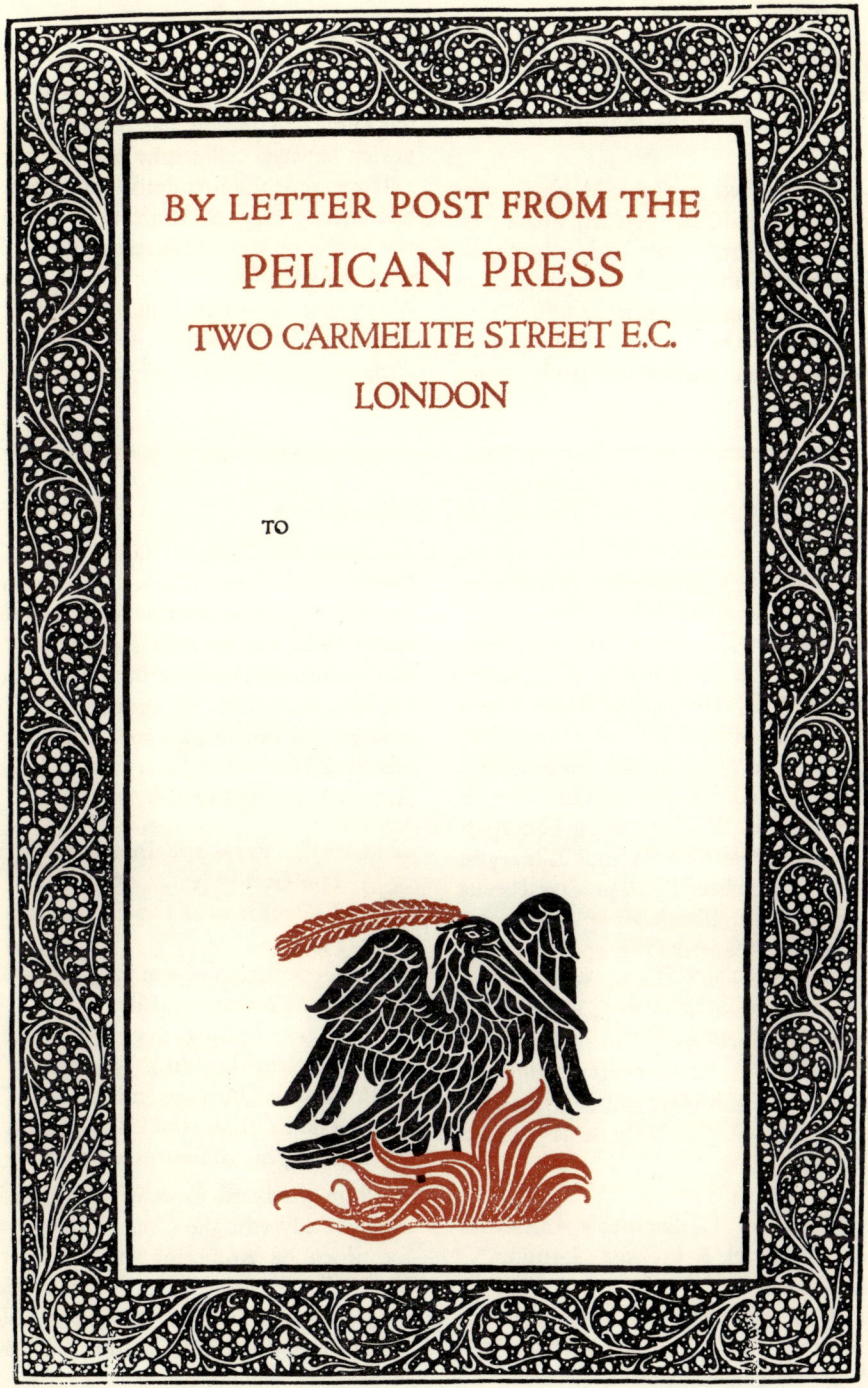

BY LETTER POST FROM THE
PELICAN PRESS
TWO CARMELITE STREET E.C.
LONDON

TO

18 *Envelope* 12 × 18 in.

20. 'The craft of printing: notes on the history of type forms, etc.' London, printed and sold at the Pelican Press, 1921

Before he left the Pelican Press Morison produced this 20-page publicity booklet, which was also his first published contribution to typographical studies. Written before the publication of D. B. Updike's *Printing types: a study in survivals*, 1922, it was 'the writer's initial effort to outline for his own satisfaction the nature of the tools he was using as "layout artist" at the Pelican Press; to determine the relation of Caslon and the Didots to Jenson and Aldus, and the connexion between calligraphy and typography'.

It was thus the first draft of an inquiry which had already engaged Morison for ten years and was to occupy him for the rest of his life. *The craft of printing*, re-written for the Cloister Press *Manchester Guardian* Printing Supplement, 23 May 1922 [23], reached its definitive form in *Type designs of the past and present*, 1925 [34].

THE CLOISTER PRESS

Charles W. Hobson, a Manchester advertising agent and a customer of the Pelican Press, set up the Cloister Press at Heaton Mersey near Manchester to specialize in printing of 'quality, atmosphere and style'. He engaged Walter Lewis previously of the Ballantyne Press as manager, and later took on Morison as typographical adviser. Morison and his wife moved north in 1921 where he found little to interest him apart from his work and the John Rylands Library in Manchester. The Cloister Press produced some outstanding display and book work.

Early in 1922 the Cloister Press opened a London office in St Stephen's House, Westminster. When in the autumn of 1922 the Cloister Press ran into financial difficulties and the original staff was dispersed, Walter Lewis became Printer to the University of Cambridge, and Morison took over the office in St Stephen's House as premises for *The Fleuron*.

21. R. C. K. Ensor: 'Catherine: a romantic poem'. Sidgwick & Jackson: London, 1921
— Publishers' note on the types used in 'Catherine'   (*Lent by John Dreyfus Esq.*)

Frank Sidgwick had this book printed in 'Garamond' [58a]; Morison provided an accompanying leaflet based on the authorities of the time. He made a mistake in attributing the initiation of the Garamond revival to Bruce Rogers; Rogers pointed this out to him and Morison promptly admitted his error to Henry Lewis Bullen of the American Type Founders Company.

22. Cloister Press specimen sheets, 1921–22
   1 The Goudy letter, 1921.
   2 A specimen of the Garamond type, 1921.
   3 A specimen of the Cloister type (n.d.).
   4 The Forum capitals, 1922.
   5 Typographical decoration and illustration (n.d.).
   6 Caslon Old face (n.d.).
   7 The English Black Letter (n.d.).
   8 A display of fleurons, ornaments, 1922.

Morison produced a set of four-leaved broadsheets to advertise the Cloister Press's resources, for which he wrote the explanatory text and Horace Taylor provided most of the illustrations.

'A display of fleurons' on the two inside pages summarizes the results of Morison's researches into printers' flowers since his cheerfully unsystematic use of them at Burns & Oates. Dr Peter Jessen, director of the Library of the Berlin Kunstgewerbe-Museum, had helped and encouraged Morison's studies, and in his book *Der Ornamentstich*, Berlin, 1920, had first shown Morison a coherent history of ornament.

23. **'The craft of printing. A brief survey of the progress and present state of the printing arts.' 'Manchester Guardian' Printing Supplement, 23 May 1922**

This supplement was edited by Charles Hobson in conjunction with Holbrook Jackson, editor of the literary monthly *Today*, and author of *The Eighteen Nineties*, who wrote most of the text.

Morison assisted in the design, and wrote the two-page note on the form of printing types. It was printed from type, not from plates, in Monotype Plantin.

24. **Letter from Morison to Oliver Simon, dated St Stephen's House, Westminster, 23 May 1922** (*Lent by Mrs Timothy Simon*)

'Dear fellow worker in the Vineyard', Morison addresses Simon. Simon, in *Printer and playground*, 1956, said that the letter was 'the first I received from Stanley Morison (who, incidentally in the last line, confirms the impression of perpetual high summer in these days of our youth) and is an example of one of his early calligraphic hands'.

25. **'Old face' in 'The Monotype Recorder', vol. xxi, no. 187, January–February 1922, pp. 4, 5** (*Lent by John Carter Esq.*)

From 1922 on the Monotype Corporation had each issue of their house journal, *The Monotype Recorder*, produced by a printing firm who used Monotype machines. Morison designed and supervised the printing of the Cloister Press's issue. He wrote this historical note introducing the Monotype series of Caslon Old Face in which the issue was set. This was the first of Morison's many contributions to *The Monotype Recorder*.

26. **'Sixe idillia, that is, Sixe small or petty poems, or aeglogues, chosen out of the right famous Sicilian poet Theocritus, and translated into English verse.' (With decorations designed and cut on wood by Vivien Gribble.) Duckworth: London, 1923**
   — **Trial sheets of 'Bucoliastae' and 'Cyclops'** (*Lent by John Dreyfus Esq.*)

Before it was decided to set the poems in Cloister Old Style, seven trial sheets were composed under Morison's direction:

'Bucoliastae'
(a) Caslon Black-letter   (c) Cloister Old Style
(b) Cloister Bold   (with Plantin italic)
'Cyclops'
(a) Cloister Old Style   (c) Cloister Old Style
(b) Goudy Modern   (d) Cloister Old Style

In the summer of 1922 Holbrook Jackson, Francis Meynell, Bernard Newdigate, and Oliver Simon (of the Curwen Press) met Morison at the London office of the Cloister Press to consider Simon's proposal for a publishing society. The proposed society would produce one book a year 'to demonstrate...that books set by machines could be as beautiful as the books of the private hand-presses'. Francis Meynell suggested the name 'The Fleuron Society'. At the two meetings which followed Newdigate upheld the superiority of the hand-set book, and so the Society was dissolved. Meynell went on to carry out Simon's intention at the Nonesuch Press; Morison and Simon decided instead to launch a new periodical, which they called *The Fleuron: a journal of typography*. By this time the Cloister Press was in liquidation and Morison had no regular employment, apart from his part-time position with the Monotype Corporation; *The Fleuron*, it was hoped, would supplement his income.

Each of the members of the abortive society contributed an article to *The Fleuron* no. 1. A few books, mostly limited editions, were published between 1924 and 1930 under the imprint of The Fleuron Limited, most of them printed at the Curwen Press.

Numbers 1–4 (1923–25) of *The Fleuron* were edited by Oliver Simon, published from the office of *The Fleuron*, St Stephen's House, Westminster, and printed by the Curwen Press. Numbers 5–7 (1926, 1928, 1930) were edited by Morison, printed by the Cambridge University Press, and published by Cambridge in England and by Doubleday in the U.S.A.

27. 'On type faces. Examples of the use of type for the printing of books: with an introductory essay and notes.'

Published jointly by the Medici Society and The Fleuron, 1923. (Printed at the Riccardi Press)

(Lent by John Carter Esq.)

The copy shown belonged to Sir Francis Meynell, who gave it to the present owner. It contains notes in Meynell's hand. There is a showing of twenty-six current faces, selected by Morison, some for hand and some for machine composition.

'The introduction is composed in 14 point Riccardi, designed by Herbert P. Horne in 1909 for Philip Lee Warner. The text is set without paragraphing, an experiment not repeated by S.M. These specimens were prepared immediately before the publication of D. B. Updike, *Printing types* (2 vols., Harvard, 1922) which the author presented to S.M., who reviewed it in *The Fleuron*, 1923. The book was the personal "Study in survivals" of a supremely sagacious, experienced and studious printer, well-rooted in the tradition of exact composition and careful machining. In consequence Updike was admirably balanced and richly suggestive and S.M. is deeply indebted to *Printing types*, as to De Vinne's *The practice of typography*.'

Morison had already been in correspondence with Daniel Berkeley Updike (1860–1941) and had sent him, at his request, the Pelican Press broadside [18], proofs of a set of the Pelican Press initials, and later the Cloister Press *Manchester Guardian* Supplement [23] and the Cloister Press specimens [22]. *Printing types*, a historical survey, based on lectures given before 1916, ignores the existence of mechanical composition and of the professional typographic adviser. Updike later became Morison's closest friend in the U.S.A., and was the first printer to import matrices of Times New Roman into America.

28. **Memorandum from Morison to Frederic and Beatrice Warde, 10 July 1925, concerning 'The Fleuron'**
(*Lent by Nicolas Barker Esq.*)

Morison proposes that recent typographical literature and recent typefounding should be comprehensively reviewed in *The Fleuron*, and that contributions should be 'written from the same angle, or the journal will degenerate into a bag of bones'.

29. **(a) Letter from Morison to Oliver Simon, Berlin, 18 October 1922**
(*Lent by Mrs Timothy Simon*)

Morison suggests the name 'The Fleuron' for the new journal.

(b) Letter from Morison to Simon, Berlin, 22 October 1922
(*Lent by Mrs Timothy Simon*)

Morison suggests a series of books to be issued by *The Fleuron* which remained unpublished. The proposed 'general editor of such a series' is unknown.

30. **'Towards an ideal type' in 'The Fleuron', no. 2, 1924, pp. 57–75**

'A formal criticism of [William] Morris's teaching, then accepted by most commentators, that Jenson's was the perfect roman, and an attempt to demonstrate, by appeal to the calligraphers of the Italian Renaissance, the right relation of the capitals to the lower case...This was the beginning of S.M.'s study of the chancery cursive.'

In the course of the article Morison writes: 'It is essential that not only should every combination of lower case letters achieve due evenness of line and colour, but that the upper case be equally homogeneous, and as easily as possible merge with the small letters.' He cites the practice of the Italian writing masters who made the tops of their capitals range below the ascenders of their minuscules.

31. **A. F. Johnson and Stanley Morison: 'The Chancery types of Italy and France' in 'The Fleuron', no. 3, 1924, pp. 23–51**

Citing the use of an upright, not sloped, type version of the italic in certain books printed in Italy in the sixteenth century, Morison makes two assertions: that slope is not an essential feature of a cursive, i.e. italic, type; and that the italics of Ludovico degli Arrighi offered 'a thoroughly practical starting point for the designing of an ideal cursive...harmonious with our classical Old faces'.

32. **'On script types' in 'The Fleuron', no. 4, 1925, pp. 1–(42)**

'A re-working of material, already collected, bringing together new illustrations documenting the career and offspring of the chancery cursive in calligraphical and typographical form. For the first time the later writing-masters, French and English, are studied and evaluated in terms of their effects upon typefounders.'

33. **'Towards an ideal italic' in 'The Fleuron', no. 5, 1926, pp. 93–129**
(*Lent by John Carter Esq.*)

This is 'an argument favouring the reduction of the cursive, and the increase of the inscriptional element in the design of italic'. The essential quality of italic, Morison asserts, is not slope but a certain informality. Before the mid-sixteenth century italic was used independently to set whole pages. It then began to be used for those parts of a text set in roman requiring emphasis or distinction – something which ought to be done with the least possible disturbance to the rest of the page. The roman type, in which the main part of the text is set, must be dominant. The associated but subordinate italic must, in the interests of harmony, lose its essential feature – informality – and most of its cursive quality.

Slope, however, though historically incidental,

is something which readers are by now so accustomed to in an italic that this feature must be retained. 'The perfect italic is therefore a slanted roman.'

Morison's theory was put into practice. Felicity, the italic to accompany Eric Gill's Perpetua [70], is basically a sloped roman. Morison also carried Jan van Krimpen with him: the Dutch type designer made a sloped roman instead of a traditional italic face for Romulus. Both he and Morison later agreed that flexibility was needed in the application of the 'sloped roman' theory.

34. 'Type designs of the past and present.'
     A double number of 'The Monotype
     Recorder', September–October and
     November–December 1925. (Printed at
     the Cambridge University Press)
                    (Lent by John Carter Esq.)
This 'sketch of the development of letter-design', as Morison called it in the preface, established his reputation as a scholar, and formed 'an essential preliminary to his work for the Monotype Corporation, and the basis of the *Memorandum* that urged *The Times* to re-design' [116].

35. 'The italic types of Antonio Blado and
     Ludovico Arrighi, printers to the

Roman Chancery' in 'The Monotype
Recorder', vol. xxvi, no. 217, January–
February   (Lent by John Carter Esq.)
This unsigned article of 20 pages occupies the whole issue, which was printed by the Cambridge University Press. Specimens of Monotype Blado and Poliphilus types were loosely inserted.

36. Denis Tegetmeier: 'No reprieve'.
     Hand-coloured etching, 1931
                (Lent by Denis Tegetmeier Esq.)
Morison is shown strangling *The Fleuron*. This is a proof which was taken by the artist while working on the plate. The whole edition was hand-coloured and amounted to about 20 prints. Morison in his 'Postscript' to the last number of *The Fleuron* wrote: 'The justification for the 1500 pages in which *The Fleuron* has discussed typography – that admittedly minor technicality of civilized life – is not the elaboration therein of the elements of arrangement, any precising of the lessons of history, though these may have been attempted; but rather its disposition to enquire, and its conviction that the teaching and example of its predecessors of the English private press left typography, as *The Fleuron* leaves it, matter for further argument.'

'FIRST PRINCIPLES OF TYPOGRAPHY'

The form in which the most internationally influential of all Morison's writings first appeared was the article 'Typography' in the *Encyclopaedia Britannica*, 1929. It was reconsidered and entirely re-written for *The Fleuron*, no. 7. The essay was first printed in book form in 1936 [39]. It has since then been republished in a considerable number of editions and translations, of which a selection is shown here.

John Johnson, Printer to the University of Oxford (1925–46), called Morison's famous essay 'the pocket testament of the craft'. In it Morison defined typography as 'the art of rightly disposing printing material in accordance with specific purpose; of so arranging the letters, distributing the space and controlling the type as to aid to the maximum the reader's comprehension of the text'. John Dreyfus (*Signature*, May 1947, p. 15) recorded Morison's settled opinion that 'the typography of serious books needed to be serious: free, at least, from diversion or distraction...The task of the designer of such books was limited to establishing general conventions that could be applied by anybody to particular books. Typographic design, in this sense, was not so much one of the graphic arts as a branch of editing.'

37. 'Typography' in 'The Encyclopaedia Britannica', 14th edition, Chicago and London, 1929

38. 'First principles of typography' in 'The Fleuron', no. 7, 1930, pp. 61–72

39. 'First principles of typography.' New York: The Macmillan Company, 1936
      (*Lent by John Carter Esq.*)
Morison in his 'Preface' wrote: 'This edition is printed at the request of American correspondents...As the brevity of the essay seems to be one of its most approved qualities, no expansion and only slight revision has been made.' One of Morison's American correspondents, Bruce Rogers, described the essay as 'the clearest and most closely reasoned exposition of the subject that I know'.

40. 'First principles of typography.' Cambridge, at the University Press, 1936   (*Lent by John Carter Esq.*)
This first Cambridge printing was published in November 1936. The edition published at Cambridge in May 1936 was printed in the U.S.A.

41. 'First principles of typography.' Amsterdam, 1946. Printed by Joh. Enschedé en Zonen, Haarlem for A. A. Balkema's Five Pound Press
   (a) Layout in pen and ink by Jan van Krimpen for the title page.
   (b) Proofs of the title page and first page of the text (p. 7) with manuscript annotations and additions by Morison.
   (c) Two trial pulls of the title page, showing Morison's name in different sizes.
   (d) Letter from Morison to Jan van Krimpen, dated London, 11 January 1946.   (*Lent by John Dreyfus Esq.*)
Designed by Jan van Krimpen, and printed in his Romulus type; twelve copies were provided with new title pages to meet Morison's comment that his name was too prominent. Morison never ceased to analyse and correct his own work; here is a slight example of his habit of amending and amplifying proofs.

42. 'Grondbeginselen van de typografie.' Utrecht: W. de Haan, 1951
      (*Lent by A. J. Gelderblom Esq.*)
The design and translation are both by Jan van Krimpen, who added a postscript of his own.

43. 'Typografiens grundlæggende principper.' København: Fagskolen for Boghaandværk, 1953
      (*Lent by John Carter Esq.*)
This translation by C. Volmer Nordlunde is set in Monotype Bembo. An earlier Danish translation – the first translation from English – by Ejnar Philip had appeared in 1949 as a publication of the Grafisk Cirkel.

44. 'Grundregeln der Typographie.' (Übertragen von Arno Krause) Berlin: Carl Heymanns Verlag, 1955
      (*Lent by John Carter Esq.*)
This first German translation, printed at the Gallus-Druckerei, Berlin, in Monotype Centaur, was made from the English text of the 1946 Amsterdam edition [41], and revised by Jan Tschichold.

45. 'Principios fundamentales de la tipo-
grafía.' (Traducción por José Aguilar)
Madrid: Aguilar, 1957
                        (*Lent by John Carter Esq.*)

46. 'Les premiers principes de la typographie' in 'Stanley Morison et la
tradition typographique', Bruxelles,
1966
— Exhibition posters

The catalogue of the exhibition 'Stanley Morison
et la tradition typographique', held in 1966 in the
Bibliothèque Albert Ier, Brussels, and the Rijks-
museum Meermanno-Westreenianum, at The
Hague, contained a French translation by Fer-
nand Baudin of *First principles of typography*.
This translation was followed by a 'Postface' by
Morison dated 5 August 1965, a shortened version
of the 'Postscript' which later appeared in English
in the 1967 Cambridge edition of *First principles*
[47]. The Dutch-language edition of the exhibition catalogue contained a new translation (with
the 'Postscript') by Huib van Krimpen, Jan van
Krimpen's son.

47. 'First principles of typography.'
Second edition. Cambridge, at the

University Press, 1967. (Cambridge
Authors' and Printers' Guides, no. 1)

In this edition, set in Monotype Bell, Morison's
'Postscript' to *First principles of typography*
appeared in full. 'It is as an exercise in the
reasoned application of experience to the art of
typography that the text here was first written;
and it is because the author's position has not
changed and his reasoning still appears to him
logical that there seems to have been no need for
alteration during the past thirty years or to-day…
The appeals to experience and reason, indeed, are
the only "traditional" factors in *First principles*.'

48. 'Grundregeln der Buchtypographie.'
Bern, 1966. (Fünfter Angelus Druck)

The editors and publishers of the Angelus
Drucke, Max Caflisch and Kurt Gschwend, made
a new translation which Morison checked, and
for which he authorized certain explanations
and annotations where they might be helpful in a
German-language edition. At the editors' request
he also supplied a version of the 'Postscript', sub-
stantially expanded for German-speaking readers.
Set in Monotype Dante and designed by Caflisch,
the book was published in an edition of 150 copies.

'THE FANFARE'

At the beginning of 1925 Charles Hobson brought
his advertising agency to London; although his
connexions with the Cloister Press had ceased he
still wanted a print workshop for his own and
other work. It was Morison who persuaded Hobson to invite Frederic and Beatrice Warde to come
to England, which led to the establishment early
in 1925 of the Fanfare at 41 Bedford Square. The
Fanfare had the dual purpose of setting Hobson's
advertisements and of producing some dis-

tinguished printing under the guidance of
Frederic Warde and Morison. (See nos. 50 and
112.) The printer at the Fanfare press was Ernest
Ingham, who continued a programme of high-
quality printing when the Fanfare was sold in
1926 to the London Press Exchange. Frederic
Warde returned to the U.S.A. in October 1927
to work with Bruce Rogers; Beatrice remained in
England to manage the publicity of the Monotype Corporation.

49. Letter from Morison to Robert Bridges, dated no. 11 Hollyberry Lane, Hampstead, October 22, 1923

(Lent by Lord Bridges)

Morison's letter, inquiring about the extent of Bridges' own part in the design and printing of his works by the Oxford University Press, was the beginning of a friendship which lasted until Bridges' death in 1930. Bridges, his wife and Morison all shared an enthusiasm for italic handwriting and for typography, in particular for printers' flowers and the Fell types. Bridges, poet laureate from 1912 to 1930, was interested in all matters connected with the craft of poetry: in prosody, versification, pronunciation and phonetic spelling. As Morison suspected, he took the business of putting his work into print very seriously.

50. Robert Bridges: 'The Tapestry'. Poems. London, privately printed, 1925

Morison obtained Bridges' permission to publish a limited edition of eleven of Bridges' latest poems, which was already in hand with the Oxford University Press (eventually published in December 1925 as *New Verse*). The 'Printer's note' states: 'For a first presentation of our new cursive type, Mr Bridges has generously authorized the printing of the following complete collection up to the present date of all his "New Verse", entitled *The Tapestry*.' Morison's new cursive type face was in fact based on Ludovico degli Arrighi's first italic of 1524. Arrighi's original type contained two forms of the letter 'g', and Morison and Warde accordingly provided for *The Tapestry* a variant design, so that there would be one letter for the hard 'g' and one for the soft. 150 copies were printed by Frederic Warde and Ernest Ingham at the Fanfare.

51. Blosius Palladius: 'Coryciana'. Rome, 1524

Ludovico degli Arrighi, formerly a scribe in the college of writers of Apostolic briefs in the Roman Curia, became a printer in 1524, in association with Lautizio Perugino, an engraver of seals, who was probably his punch-cutter. His first printed book, *Coryciana*, is a collection of Latin poems in honour of Johannes Goritz, Protonotary Apostolic, edited by Blossio Palladio, one of the Papal secretaries, and printed in an italic face designed by Arrighi and based on the chancery cursive hand. This italic is very different from the earlier italic of Aldus Manutius, has few ligatures, and shows the beginnings of true italic capitals.

52. 'The calligraphic models of Ludovico degli Arrighi surnamed Vicentino. A complete facsimile (of La Operina, 1522, and Il modo di temperare le penne, 1523) and introduction.' Paris, privately printed for Frederic Warde, 1926. 300 copies printed at the Officina Bodoni, Montagnola
— Prospectus

(Lent by the Curators of the Bodleian Library)

Arrighi's writing-books did much to spread the *cancellaresca corsiva*, of which he was a master. *La Operina*, printed from engraved woodblocks, gave instructions with specimens; his second book included other hands too.

Morison used the new type to set his introduction. He commended Arrighi's chancery hand to 'moderns in search of a base for simple and legible current hands'; and pointed out that it was on Arrighi's italic types, and not the Aldine, that the italics of Garamond and Caslon were modelled.

53. **Robert Bridges: 'The influence of the audience'. New York, Garden City. One hundred copies printed for Stanley Morison at the press of Doubleday, Page & Co., 1926**

54. **Robert Bridges: 'The influence of the audience on Shakespeare's drama'. (Collected Essays, Papers &c of Robert Bridges. Vol. 1.) Oxford University Press: London, 1927**

In 1926 one hundred copies of Bridges' Shakespearean essay *The influence of the audience* were printed by Morison at the Garden City Press of Doubleday, the New York publishers. *The influence of the audience* appeared again in 1927 as the first volume of the Oxford University Press edition of Bridges' *Collected Essays* with the first four of the poet's planned series of phonotypes, designed by Morison and cut by the Monotype Corporation. The typography of this little book embodies most of Morison's theories about design as well as some of Bridges' on spelling. It was set throughout in Blado italic, 13 point for text and 10 point for footnotes, with Poliphilus 16 point small capitals instead of the normal italic capitals, in the manner of Aldus Manutius. Four more of Bridges' phonotypes followed in the next volume, published in 1928.

On this copy of Morison's edition of *The influence of the audience* Bridges indicated where his phonetic symbols were to be used in the Oxford University Press edition.

55. **Robert Bridges: 'The Testament of Beauty'. Oxford, 1927–1929**

First trial text, corrected by the author. Presented by the author to Morison and by Morison to the British Museum.

56. **Robert Bridges: 'The Testament of Beauty'. A poem in four books. Oxford, at the Clarendon Press, 1929**

In 1926 Bridges started the great work of his old age, *The Testament of Beauty*. Morison was one of those he asked to read and criticize the poem, in a preliminary private edition set in Fell English roman printed by the Clarendon Press in an edition of 25 copies. Morison in a pencil note records that he lost his copy of Book I of the trial text, and that to replace the loss Bridges in 1930 gave him this copy corrected in his own hand, from which the limited quarto edition was printed by the Clarendon Press.

Morison was responsible for the design of the quarto edition published on 24 October 1929, the day after Bridges' 85th birthday, printed in a new large size (16 point) of Bembo.

THE MONOTYPE CORPORATION

For four centuries after the invention of printing, type was set by hand using a composing stick, a slow process which required considerable quantities of pre-cast type. Throughout the nineteenth century inventors sought ways of performing this task by machine. It was the American Linn Boyd Benton's invention in 1885 of a pantographic punch-cutting and matrix-engraving machine that enabled hot-metal composing machines to be supplied with matrices in sufficient quantities for mechanical composition. Two hot-metal composing machines were successfully developed, again by American inventors: Ottmar Mergenthaler in 1886 patented his matrix composing, line-justifying and line-casting machine, Linotype, which casts whole lines of type as one piece;

Tolbert Lanston patented in 1887 the Monotype machine for casting, composing and justifying single types, a process regarded in this country as especially suitable for book work.

The Monotype machine was demonstrated in London for the first time in 1897. After fire had destroyed the Monotype factory in America the whole enterprise might well have failed if a British syndicate had not provided capital. The newly formed Lanston Monotype Corporation* in London purchased from the Lanston Monotype Machine Company of Philadelphia the entire rights for every country outside North and South America. Understandably the Monotype engineers at this stage concentrated on technical rather than aesthetic improvement. Still, they had in 1911 cut Veronese, a face based on a fifteenth-century original, for the publisher J. M. Dent's Everyman's Library series.

In 1913, as we have seen, the Monotype Corporation cut Imprint for Gerard Meynell and J. H. Mason; and in the same year issued its first contribution to jobbing typography, Plantin, based on types preserved in the Plantin-Moretus Museum at Antwerp.

In 1916 the Corporation had started to cut a faithful copy of the original Caslon. Despite advances in technique, it is generally true to say that by the end of the First World War it was considered sound business to cut new faces only in response to demand from customers, and not to produce new faces to attract orders.

Morison could not show the Monotype engineers (who had already produced Imprint, Caslon and Plantin with conspicuous skill) anything about the techniques of cutting of letters for mechanical composition. What he did was to prepare in 1922 for the consideration of the managing director, Harold M. Duncan (an American

* The name was changed in 1931 to the Monotype Corporation Limited. The word Monotype is a registered trade mark, by permission used in this catalogue without quotes.

interested in better type faces), a comprehensive programme of type design to be developed ahead of demand, together with a supporting programme of education and publicity. Later in the same year Morison was appointed typographical adviser to the Monotype Corporation, 'on the understanding' (as he explained in *A tally of types*, 1953, p. 9) 'that the matrix cutting and publicity programme... would be proceeded with immediately'.

Duncan's successor, William Burch, confirmed both Duncan's decision and Morison's appointment. Morison's plan provided in the first place that a number of new book faces in the usual sizes should be cut in succession. The sales of types produced in the first six years more than justified the venture in terms of cash, and Monotype's competitors (the makers of founders' type and of other machine composition systems) often followed with their versions of faces revived in the Monotype programme. That programme is described by Brooke Crutchley, Printer to Cambridge University, as 'a highly successful industrial venture, by which Britain (i.e. Morison) wrested from the United States and Germany the leadership in typographical design'.

GARAMOND

In the programme of type design adopted by the Monotype Corporation in 1922 a face of French Renaissance origin was given first place. The Monotype Garamond roman was derived from a contemporary print taken off the presses of the Imprimerie Nationale, Paris, who had early this century revived the use of some types in their possession called the '*caractères de l'université*', then wrongly attributed to the great sixteenth-century punch-cutter Claude Garamond. In recutting this design, the Monotype Corporation had been anticipated by the American Type Founders Company, the first typefounders to have a special type design department, who in

1917 had brought out a version which they called 'Garamond' and which had met with great success. William Burch, then secretary of the Monotype Corporation, decided to have a version of 'Garamond' cut for machine composition.

The italic was cut first in 1922. This highly ligatured face, the like of which had not hitherto been produced for mechanical composition – a technical triumph of the punch-cutting machine – was followed by the roman in 1923. In *A tally of types* Morison maintained that he had been able to secure that Monotype Garamond italic would reproduce, not the italic of the *caractères de l'université*, but the biggest of those in the specimen of the Imprimerie Royale, 1643, which is now known to be the 'Gros Canon cursive' cut by Robert Granjon.

57. **The Monotype Corporation: broadsheet type specimen: 'Garamond, a type face in eight sizes of roman and italic'**
     (*Lent by the Monotype Corporation*)
The Monotype Corporation issued some fine publicity explaining their new type faces.

58. **(a) American Type Founders Company: 'Claude Garamond: the first type founder' 1921. (Formerly in Morison's possession)**
    (b) Photographs of pages from 'Épreuves générales des caractères qui se trouvent chez Claude Lamesle', Paris, 1742
    Gros Romain ordinaire no. xlv.
    Gros Romain italique ordinaire no. xlvi.
    Gros Canon maîgre ordinaire no. lviii.
    Gros Canon italique maîgre ordinaire no. lix.
    (Formerly in Morison's possession)
    (c) Letter from Morison to Sydney Caslon, Chairman of the Caslon Letter Foundry, 19 September 1921
     (*Lent by John Dreyfus Esq.*)

In this letter to Sydney Caslon Morison states his preference for some of the sixteenth-century romans and italics shown by Lamesle, as against any of the revived 'Garamond' letters.

A. F. Johnson in his introduction to the facsimile edition of 1965 of Lamesle's specimen book confirms that the 'Oeil ordinaire' in all sizes is indeed a Garamond face, either the original or a close copy.

59. **Paul Beaujon, i.e. Mrs Beatrice Warde: 'The Garamond types' in 'The Fleuron', no. 5, 1926, pp. 131–79**
     (*Lent by John Carter Esq.*)
When Mrs Warde's article on the 'Garamond' types was about to be printed, she came across a page in the Bagford collection of title-pages in the British Museum which was printed by Jean Jannon of Sedan. 'There staring me in the face was the type I had been searching for.' That night she took the boat to Paris to consult the unique copy of Jannon's specimen book in the Mazarine library. Under her pseudonym she published in the amended article her discovery that it was Jannon, in the seventeenth century, cut off by the religious wars from supplies of type from the Egenolff foundry, who had cut the *caractères de l'université*. The Monotype Corporation offered 'Paul Beaujon' a job, and Mrs Warde became editor of *The Monotype Recorder*. She took over and expanded the publicity work which Morison had started.

BASKERVILLE

John Baskerville, writing master and printer, was born in Birmingham in 1706. He printed and published editions of the classics notable for the fineness of the materials he used, the sobriety and refinement of his book design and the type face he designed, which was appreciated more on the Continent than in England. In 1779 the French playwright Beaumarchais bought Baskerville's typographical material to print his famous edition of the works of Voltaire between 1784 and 1789.

The Monotype recutting of Baskerville issued in 1923 took as a model for all sizes the Great Primer design used by Baskerville in his finest books, the quarto classics and the folio Bible. Its success has proved permanent. Baskerville and Bembo appear more often than any other faces in the National Book League's annual exhibition of British book production.

60. The Monotype Corporation: broadsheet type specimen: 'Specimen of printing letter designed by John Baskerville about the year 1757'
   (Lent by the Monotype Corporation)

61. 'The Baskerville types. A critique' (by Stanley Morison and Beatrice Warde) in 'The Monotype Recorder', vol. xxvi, no. 221, September–October 1927, pp. 3–27   *(Lent by John Carter Esq.)*
This critique constitutes the whole text of the issue. It is set in and followed by specimens of Monotype Baskerville, 'reproduced accurately from the original Baskerville types rather than from the modified versions of his successors', i.e. the Great Primer type as used by John Baskerville in his edition of Terence of 1773. In fact the Monotype version regularizes the cut of the letters, the intention being to accord rather with Baskerville's design than with his punch-cutter's rendering of it.

Morison himself said that the salient feature of the article was the analysis by Beatrice Warde of the contrast between the angle of shading of the round character as between Old face and Modern face. Hitherto it had been held that the difference lay only in the serif-construction and the relation of thicks and thins.

FOURNIER AND BARBOU

Two trial founts were cut in 1924 for a roman and italic derived from the early work of the great eighteenth-century French printer and typecutter Pierre-Simon Fournier, or Fournier-le-jeune, both based on his Saint-Augustin Ordinaire cut by Fournier before 1742. Morison preferred the thicker, darker version because its heavier thick strokes produced a darker-coloured page. While Morison was abroad work proceeded in error on the lighter version, which was issued as Monotype Fournier.

Of the second design, which Morison preferred, only one size in one set of matrices was struck. They were acquired by the Cambridge University Press and named 'Barbou' after a French printer who made use of Fournier's types. It was not until 1959 that another size was cut for *The Papers of Benjamin Franklin*, Yale University Press, printed by the Lakeside Press, Chicago; Franklin himself had printed with the types of Pierre-Simon Fournier.

The original set of Barbou matrices was used for the composition of the last three numbers of *The Fleuron*, edited by Morison, and printed by the Cambridge University Press.

62. The Monotype Corporation: broadsheet type specimen: Fournier
   (Lent by the Monotype Corporation)

63. The Monotype Corporation: 'Almanack 1929. With twelve designs on wood by Eric Ravilious and a specimen of the Roman and Italic of Fournier-le-jeune composed on the Monotype'
   (Lent by John Dreyfus Esq.)
Of the *Almanack*, an erudite compilation devised by Mrs Warde, the month of May is shown, and at the head of the second page the entry for 6 May, Morison's birthday and the feast of St John before the Latin Gate, patron saint of scribes and printers.

64. **The Double Crown Club: The fifth dinner of the Double Crown Club. Wednesday, October 28 1925 at the Criterion Restaurant (Menu)**
(Lent by the Curators of the Bodleian Library)
The engraving *au burin* is by J. E. Laboureur. 'The letterpress is the first use of a reproduction of Fournier-le-jeune's *St Augustin*, the property of S. Morison. 75 copies printed for him by Walter Lewis at the University Press, Cambridge.'

The Double Crown Club was founded in 1924 by Oliver Simon and Hubert Foss 'for the purpose of exchanging ideas on good printing'. Morison was an original member of the committee and had by 1956 read more papers at the Club's meetings than any other member.

POLIPHILUS AND BLADO
The idea of reproducing the type used by Aldus Manutius for the *Hypnerotomachia Poliphili* (1499) came from Harry Lawrence of the publishing firm of Lawrence & Bullen. By 1923 he had provided the Monotype Corporation with the sheets from a broken copy of the book; individual letters were photographically enlarged as patterns for the pantographic engravers who reproduced every detail faithfully. It was not at the time realized that this accurate facsimile of the letters on particular pages was likely to prove less satisfactory than a re-creation of the intended appearance of the types when unworn. Morison pointed out that to redraw, not merely to reproduce, an ancient original available only in the form of contemporary print (i.e. when no original matrices, punches or types survive) was more difficult than direct imitation.

For Blado, the companion italic, Morison rejected the Aldine italic and adapted by a slight change in slope a design of Ludovico degli Arrighi's used by the Roman printer Antonio Blado, itself a type version of the Roman chancery script.

The first book printed in Poliphilus was Morison's *Four centuries of fine printing*, 1924 [83].

65. **The Monotype Corporation: two broadsheet type specimens for Poliphilus**

66. **The Monotype Corporation: two broadsheet type specimens for Blado italic**   *(Lent by the Monotype Corporation)*

NEW HELLENIC
67. Αἰσώπου τοῦ μυθοποίου λόγοι ἕπτα. **Text composed in the New Hellenic designed by Victor Scholderer and cut by the Lanston Monotype Corporation, London. The engravings by David Jones. The translations by W. H. Shewring. London, 1928**
(Lent by John Dreyfus Esq.)
Morison wanted a Greek type satisfactory for ordinary use (unlike, for example, Gill's unaccented and seriffed Perpetua Greek). Victor Scholderer of the British Museum, on behalf of a committee of the Society for the Promotion of Hellenic Studies, designed New Hellenic, a sans-serif face. The lower case was adapted from the fifteenth-century Venetian face used in an edition of Macrobius, printed by Joannes Rubeus in 1492, while the capitals, absent in the original, were freshly added.

In 1927 two sizes of New Hellenic were shown in an exhibition in the British Museum illustrating the development of Greek printing types, and in a volume of facsimiles with an introduction by Victor Scholderer, *Greek printing types 1465–1927*. The first book printed in the New Hellenic was this privately printed edition of seven of Æsop's fables. This copy, presented by Morison to Ruth and Victor Gollancz, is one of fifty printed in the office of the Monotype Corporation.

GILL SANS

Morison was impressed by the practical yet beautifully shaped serifless capitals of the lettering on the sign above the Bristol bookshop of his friend Douglas Cleverdon, painted by Eric Gill. He therefore persuaded Gill to provide drawings not only for an upper case titling alphabet but also for a lower case. Gill introduced some variations in thickness: this was in order to reduce the monotony often found in lengthy passages set in the earlier sans-serif faces, in which the letters were often mechanically drawn and of geometrically consistent proportions.

Gill, an outspoken opponent of industrial methods in any work better done by hand, was at first reluctant to have his handiwork transformed by machines into types, which would then be used for printing by other machines. Morison convinced Gill that good printing was an acceptable extension of good design, with the result that Gill not only designed other types but also set himself up as a commercial printer, had his own types made and wrote about printing.

The first showing of Gill Sans was the programme Morison designed for a meeting of the Publicity and Selling Committee at the Congress of the Federation of Master Printers, 1928 [113]. Gill himself made the drawings for all the variants of Gill Sans, condensed, bold or fat; although he modified his original design following suggestions by the Monotype Type Drawing Office, the various display versions were drawn by Gill and not developed by mechanical methods.

68. The Monotype Corporation: broad-
    sheet type specimen: Gill Sans
        (*Lent by the Monotype Corporation*)

69. Photograph of the fascia of Douglas
    Cleverdon's bookshop in Bristol
    showing Gill's sans-serif lettering
        (*Lent by Douglas Cleverdon Esq.*)

PERPETUA AND FELICITY

Once the Monotype programme had proved a financial success, Morison was in a position to recommend the Corporation to risk something new: a book face commissioned from a living artist. Suspecting what Beatrice Warde called 'the fatal facility of the pantographic punch-cutter', Morison did not look to calligraphers and draughtsmen as such for a contemporary roman type suitable for commercial book work. In Morison's view only cutters of letters in stone, wood or metal could produce the fine serif ('not in origin calligraphic but epigraphic; not written but sculptured') in which lay the distinction of the work of Griffo or Fournier. He realized that what he required was drawings by a calligrapher who was also an engraver – by Eric Gill.

As early as November 1925 Gill produced some letters for Morison. From these punches were cut by hand in Paris by Charles Malin, who modified Gill's designs in those slight respects necessary to interpret them adequately in metal. The punches were struck in 1926 and trial matrices were made and type was cast by Ribadeau-Dumas, the Paris typefounders. Gill made further corrections on the smoke-proofs, and the matrices were brought to London for the Monotype engineers to use in making the matrices for machine casting. Perpetua was then issued in 1929.

Felicity, the italic to accompany Perpetua, was intended as a sloped roman, but with three upper case and three lower case characters using those cursive forms traditional in an italic face.

70. 'The Passion of Perpetua and Felicity
    martyred at Carthage A.D. CCIII.'
    A new translation by W. H. Shewring
    with engravings on wood by Eric Gill.
    Printed for 'The Fleuron': London, 1929
    Inset between pp. 50–51 of Paul Beaujon,
    'Eric Gill: sculptor of letters', in 'The
    Fleuron', VII
        (*Lent by Douglas Cleverdon Esq.*)

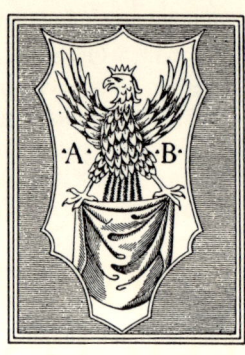

THE
ITALIC OF
ANTONIO
BLADO

THE
OFFICIAL
PRINTER
ROME

1515—1567

NOW RECUT BY
THE MONOTYPE CORPORATION LIMITED
43 AND 44, FETTER LANE, LONDON, E.C.4
ANNO DOMINI · MCMXXIV

The choice of a suitable italic to accompany the reproduction of "Monotype"
Poliphilus was not made without considerable research since it was only after the
passing of a generation or two that italic and roman were designed as two con-
stituents of one fount. The present italic is based upon the finest of the letters used
by the distinguished printer Antonio Blado who occupied the office of printer to
the Holy See during the years 1515 to 1567. In all probability this printer's types
were designed by the renowned calligrapher Ludovico Arrighi Vicentino who
held the post of writer of apostolic briefs, and they were probably cut by the
famous goldsmith of Perugia, Lautizio de Bartolomeo dei Rotelli. Blado's
italic, now made available to "Monotype" machine users, possesses a
very elegant line and a note of personality which cannot fail to fit
it for employment in the finer kinds of advertising and book-
work. In conjunction with the Poliphilus roman, printers
possess a series of great character and permanent
interest. Extra sorts for use in various kinds
of antiquarian printing have been cut
and may be incorporated without
trouble in the matrix case.

A
BCDEFG
HIJKLMNO&
PQRSTUVWXYZABC QUQV
abcdefghijklmnopq
rstuvwxyzabc
ct st sp st tt ll
sp ct st a b

THE PASSION OF

PERPETUA AND
FELICITY

MARTYRED AT CARTHAGE A.D. CCIII

A NEW TRANSLATION BY

W. H. SHEWRING

WITH ENGRAVINGS ON WOOD

BY

ERIC GILL

London, 1929

PRINTED FOR 'THE FLEURON'

in Perpetua roman made by the

Lanston Monotype Corporation from the design of

ERIC GILL

The first size, 13 point, of the upper and lower case of Monotype Perpetua was completed in August 1928 and first shown in a private print of the English translation, made for this purpose by Walter Shewring, of *The Passion of Perpetua and Felicity*. The roman was named 'Perpetua' and the italic (cut later) 'Felicity'. Morison wrote: 'Perpetua may be judged in the small sizes to have achieved the object of providing a distinguished form for a distinguished text; and, in the large sizes, a noble, monumental appearance.'

71. **The Monotype Corporation: broadsheet type specimen: Perpetua**
(*Lent by the Monotype Corporation*)

BEMBO

After the recutting of Poliphilus in 1923 Morison's typographical studies led him to consider the revival of an earlier form of the Aldine roman letter, used to print Pietro Bembo's *De Aetna* of 1495. Morison considered that 'the virtues of the book as a book, and of the type as a design can only be appreciated if more than one page, and preferably the whole, of Bembo's tract is studied ...and seen with Aldus's other productions in roman'. After comparing the letter of the *De Aetna* with that of the *Hypnerotomachia Poliphili*, 1499, he decided that the upper and lower case letters harmonized better in the earlier work. Moreover the lower case letters of the *De Aetna* were more brilliant than any cut before: possibly Francesco Griffo, Aldus's punch-cutter, had access to harder alloys than his predecessors, which enabled him to use finely cut bracketed serifs.

In recutting the type of the *De Aetna*, Morison was anxious to produce, not just a copy of the inked impressions on the pages of the Aldine prototype, but a face suitable for modern press-work on most papers; Monotype Bembo, issued in 1929, has become very widely used. In Morison's view, its Aldine model was inspired 'not by writing but by engraving; not script but

sculpture', in this respect similar to Gill's Perpetua.

There was some difficulty in finding a matching italic for Bembo. The design first proposed, based on drawings by the distinguished calligrapher, Alfred Fairbank,* had the great merit of all chancery cursives: it was legible in the mass and could be easily read by the page. 'So much so that, in fact,' wrote Morison, 'it looked happier alone than in association with the Bembo roman.' It was eventually decided to issue Fairbank's italic separately under the name of Narrow Bembo Italic (later Condensed Bembo Italic). A second italic was produced to go with Bembo, a modification of a chancery cursive hand originally reproduced in Giovanni Antonio Tagliente's *La vera arte de la excellente scrivere*, 1524. For this purpose the ascenders of Tagliente's script were seriffed, and the capitals – roman, as used by Tagliente – were mechanically sloped.

72. **Cardinal Pietro Bembo: 'De Aetna'. Venice, 1495. Leaf Aii**

73. **'Petri Bembi de Aetna liber.' English version, 'On Aetna', by Betty Radice. Editiones Officina Bodoni: Verona, 1969. In memoriam Stanley Morison**
Title page; colophon; reproduction of leaf Aii; p. 141, showing 6 lines from the original Aldus edition, 6 lines in Griffo type, 6 lines in Bembo type.

For this memorial edition, printed on the hand press of the Officina Bodoni, Dr Giovanni Mardersteig used both Monotype Bembo (for composing the English translation and postscript) and his own hand-cut version of the type of the Aldine *De Aetna*, which he called Griffo, after Aldus's punch-cutter, Francesco Griffo. In 1930 Morison had advised Mardersteig, who wanted

* See Alfred Fairbank, 'Condensed Bembo Italic', in the *Journal of the Society for Italic Handwriting*, Winter 1962, pp. 8–11.

to have a type cut by the punch-cutter Charles Malin, to take the Aldine *De Aetna* as a model. As Mardersteig explains in his postscript, 'A note on the types', Morison regretted that in the mechanical recutting of Monotype Bembo something of the supple elegance of the original had been lost. Because in the Aldine *De Aetna* the number of variations in forms of the same letter is unusually high (in imitation of calligraphic practice) it was not easy to select the best versions to follow. Moreover, variations caused by defects in the casting of the original types and blemishes through over-inking had to be corrected before making a reproduction of even an exceptionally well-printed page from Bembo's original text. It is instructive to compare the page Mardersteig reproduces in his book with the same page in a British Museum copy of the *De Aetna*; and to recall that Morison found it best to consult several copies of an exemplar in choosing the model letters for the recutting of a type.

When Morison compared the first trial setting of Griffo with Monotype Bembo he was surprised to find that the fount cut by hand was far closer to the original than the version cut for mechanical composition. 'The weight of Monotype Bembo is much more even than Griffo's cutting, and it has the advantage of being more suitable for general use because of its deviations from the original model, some of them made for technical reasons and others in order to produce a more regular appearance.' Bembo was a favourite design of Morison's, and it has remained one of the most popular Monotype faces, especially for fine printing, all over the world.

74. **British Museum: 'Catalogue of an exhibition of books illustrating British and foreign printing, 1919–1929'. London, by order of the Trustees, 1929. (Printed at the University Press, Cambridge)**

The Monotype Corporation bore the entire cost of printing this catalogue, which was compiled by Dr Henry (later Sir Henry) Thomas of the Department of Printed Books. It is the first use of Monotype Bembo.

75. **The Double Crown Club: Twenty-second dinner, 29 May 1929. Kettner's Restaurant, Soho**

This menu, after giving the bill of fare, reads: 'Mr Oliver Simon in the Chair. Dr Henry Thomas will be the guest of the Club and will talk about the Exhibition of Twentieth Century Printing at the British Museum.'

CENTAUR

76. **The Monotype Corporation: broadsheet type specimen: Centaur**
    (*Lent by the Monotype Corporation*)

Bruce Rogers, recognizing the success of Monotype Garamond and Poliphilus, offered his own design, Centaur (hand-cut in 1915 for hand-setting), to the Monotype Corporation so that it could be made available for machine composition. Centaur was modelled on the type of Nicolas Jenson's edition of Eusebius' *De evangelica praeparatione*, 1470. Rogers's redrawn version for Monotype Centaur was issued in 1929 and used in the Oxford Lectern Bible, which Rogers designed and the production of which he personally supervised – in Morison's opinion, 'the most monumental impression ever given to a Monotype face'. (The type was in fact redrawn for this book and the 22-point Centaur was recut on an 18-point body so that the type could be machine-set.)

Jenson worked before italic appeared in print; and Rogers in 1915 did not design a companion italic for Centaur. For Monotype Centaur, however, Morison's experiments (at Rogers's suggestion) began with a modified version of Arrighi, the hand-cut italic first used in 1925 to print Robert Bridges' poem *The Tapestry*.

LUTETIA

Morison sought new type faces for the Monotype Corporation from his friend, the Dutch designer Jan van Krimpen. Their correspondence and frequent meetings had begun when Morison had thanked Van Krimpen in 1926 for a review of *The Fleuron* in *Het Boek*.

In 1923 Enschedé en Zonen of Haarlem asked Van Krimpen to design a type face: two years later one size was ready for use in a guide to the Dutch section of the 'Exposition internationale des arts décoratifs et industriels modernes' held in Paris, and the type face was called Lutetia. Morison wrote to Van Krimpen to say how much he liked Lutetia, and praised it in an introduction to the catalogue of an exhibition in London of Enschedé en Zonen's work. At Morison's instigation, and by arrangement with Van Krimpen and Enschedé, a Monotype version of Lutetia was issued in 1931.

Van Krimpen had designed Lutetia for casting by hand, and later regretted that he had not modified the design to make it better suited to the unit system of the Monotype type-setting machines.

TIMES NEW ROMAN

In 1929 the advertising manager of *The Times* solicited from the Monotype Corporation a full-page advertisement in *The Times* Printing Supplement at £1000 a page, offering to write the copy and have it set up at Printing House Square by the compositors of *The Times*. When Morison heard this he said he thought it would be better to pay *The Times* £1000 not to set up any advertisement for the Corporation, because the paper was in such need of typographical reform. *The Times* management asked Morison what they should do about it and eventually appointed him as their typographical adviser. He proposed in October 1930 'that the type faces used in the editorial and advertising columns of *The Times* be re-designed and brought up to the standard of the average book as brought out by London publishers'. It was Morison's aim to provide *The Times* with a type face which, while satisfying the requirements of economy and legibility, would combine the individuality of the Old face and the brilliance of the Modern.

In September 1930 a committee was formed to consider 'the desirability of making an alteration in the present editorial and heading founts'. Among its members were the assistant editor, R. M. Barrington-Ward – a supporter of change – and Harold Child, a journalist who was also an enthusiast for good printing; but Morison was the leading spirit.

After experiments with pages set in existing newspaper faces and some Monotype book faces on a curved stereo plate, Morison's choice settled on a 'modernized Plantin' as a basis for a new type face.

The committee, in agreeing that a comprehensive new type was desirable, had stipulated that it must occupy the same space as the types already in use in *The Times* and that it must be 'square' (neither too condensed nor too expanded). Monotype Plantin, based upon a Grosse Mediane Romaine by Robert Granjon, was chosen by Morison as a point of departure, and it exactly fits this prescription: it is large for its body, with long letters correspondingly shortened, but economical in horizontal space. Drawings based on this face were prepared by Victor Lardent, a draughtsman on the staff of *The Times*, and amended under Morison's direction. The final drawings were handed to the Monotype Corporation, who cut punches and prepared specimens for three text sizes (9, 7, 5½ point) and headings.

Times New Roman first appeared in the issue of *The Times* of 3 October 1932 [120]. For a year Times New Roman was the exclusive property of *The Times*, although with the permission of the proprietors, the September/October 1932 issue of *The Monotype Recorder*, a special issue on 'The Times and its new roman type', was printed at Cambridge in the new type face. When the restriction was lifted, Times New Roman was cut for Linotype and other composing machines as well as for foundry type. Despite its origin as a newspaper face it has been found suitable for a great range of work; its utility has also been expanded by the cutting of a number of related series, including a wide version for the composing of lines longer than the short lines of narrow newspaper columns, and a semi-bold version [90]. Times New Roman has become one of the most successful and widely accepted of all type faces cut this century.

Times New Roman has a greater x-height than most other faces, i.e. the low letters of the lower case are taller than usual; the ascenders and descenders are shorter than usual. With greater x-height letters can have narrower counters and this makes for compactness and economy of space horizontally and vertically.

Times New Roman in the italic shows the influence of Morison's 'sloped roman' theory, with those concessions to the italic tradition which in his experience had been proved necessary. In Morison's words, however, it 'owes more to Didot than dogma'.

77. **The Monotype Corporation: broadsheet type specimen: Times New Roman**
(*Lent by the Monotype Corporation*)

78. **Two pen and wash alphabets drawn by Victor Lardent who also drew designs for the Times New Roman type under Morison's supervision**
(*Lent by the St Bride Printing Library*)
(a) Alphabet, with an alternative W, 1½ in. letters. Used for the new title piece of *The Times*, 3 October 1932, and evidently redrawn, where the E, H, I, M, S and T were concerned, from the first title piece of *The Times* of 1788. The remaining letters probably loosely modelled on late-eighteenth-century lettering. Used, as a drawn letter, for *The Times* publicity.

(b) Alphabet, with alternative M and W, 2 in. letters. Perhaps an early design for Times Extended Titling (Monotype series 339).

BELL

The 'Modern face' type originally cut for John Bell by Richard Austin in 1788 was used in England mainly for Bell's own newspaper *The Oracle*, described by Morison as 'the most elegant sheet ever printed'. Bell's British Letter Foundry closed in 1797, and after a while Bell's fine types were forgotten in England and not seen again until 1930. In 1864 a set of Bell's types, cast from the original matrices which had descended by purchase to the foundry of Stephenson, Blake and Co., went to America, where they were later used at the Riverside Press under the name of 'Brimmer'. The type attracted the admiration of Daniel Berkeley Updike. He obtained strikes for his own casting from Stephenson, Blake, calling his version 'Mountjoye'. Morison's chance discovery in the Bibliothèque Nationale of the unique copy of Bell's type specimen, 'Address to the World by Mr. Bell, British-Library, Strand, London', which he immediately recognized to be composed in the 'Brimmer' or 'Mountjoye' types, revealed the true origin of these American founts. The 'Address' was reproduced in Morison's *John Bell, 1745-1831* (Cambridge, 1930) [126] composed with new founts cast from the original material by Stephenson, Blake and Co. This publication, and the Bell exhibition arranged in 1931 by the First Edition Club, were advance publicity for the Monotype facsimile recutting, made with the collaboration of Stephenson, Blake. Monotype Bell was first used for the text of *The English Newspaper* (Cambridge, 1932) [132].

79. **The Monotype Corporation: broadsheet type specimen: Bell**
(*Lent by the Monotype Corporation*)

VAN DIJCK

Morison wished to add to the Monotype Corporation's list a face based on the types of Christoffel van Dijck (1601–72). Enschedé en Zonen held the only surviving typographical materials attributable to Van Dijck, the original punches and matrices of an italic; those of the corresponding roman, shown in the 1768 Enschedé specimen book, had been lost. Morison asked Van Krimpen's advice on which seventeenth-century roman faces would be best for the Monotype Corporation to adapt as a companion face for the revived Van Dijck italic. Van Krimpen doubted whether the roman shown in the 1768 specimen and the italic surviving at Haarlem were in fact by the same hand, or by Van Dijck at all. He found a book containing a roman face more likely to have come from the designer of the italic, a translation by Vondel of Ovid's *Metamorphoses* of 1671. Six trial punches for this roman were cut by Enschedé's punch-cutter P. H. Rädisch in 1934 under Van Krimpen's supervision, to provide the points of comparison required for the mechanical cutting of the founts of Monotype Van Dijck. An enlarged image of the hand-cut punch provided the pattern for the pantographically engraved punch.

Van Krimpen's own version of a roman to go with the 'Van Dijck' italic, which he called Romanée (after the Burgundy vineyard – he took the name from a wine-bottle label), was cut in 1928. It was transferred, along with some of the Romulus type family, to Monotype matrices in 1936.

ROMULUS

Between 1931 and 1937 Van Krimpen designed Romulus, a whole family of types, to provide the basic necessities of book printing in a series of related designs. Several of these founts were issued as a joint enterprise by the Monotype Corporation and Enschedé en Zonen, and a number of details show the influence of Morison's

teachings and criticism. The most important is the sloped roman instead of a cursive italic designed as the associated face [27]. There were practical difficulties in the founding, for although the angle of inclination was normal, the overhang of certain characters caused problems in the fit of the letters. Moreover, as A. F. Johnson wrote in his review of the new face in *Signature*, no. 13 (1940), 'sloped roman may be logical but results in a stiff and monotonous letter'. Both Morison and Van Krimpen later acknowledged that this experiment had not succeeded.

The main founts and sizes were issued by the Monotype Corporation in 1936, and Beatrice Warde christened this type family (from the roman) Romulus – 'for if he was not a good Roman, who was?'

ALBERTUS

Berthold Wolpe, one of the most distinguished pupils of Rudolf Koch at the Arts and Crafts School at Offenbach, was trained in a bronze foundry. He made inscriptions in relief by cutting away the background; such a technique produces bold shapes, a sharp line without angular terminals and only rudimentary serifs. Soon after Wolpe's arrival in England in 1932, Morison, who had seen photographs of his inscriptional work, commissioned from him a titling fount, which has become one of the few display faces to remain constantly in fashion. The Monotype Corporation issued the Albertus capitals in 1936, and Albertus was completed as a family with a lower case and range of sizes between 1937 and 1940.

80. **The Monotype Corporation: broadsheet type specimen: 'Albertus capitals'**

(Lent by the Monotype Corporation)

SACHSENWALD

Morison, with his interest in black-letter, took the opportunity of commissioning from Wolpe

Sachsenwald, a condensed black-letter. Sachsenwald was first shown in *The Monotype Recorder*, Spring 1937, where it appeared in headings in three sizes on the back cover, but is neither named nor credited anywhere in the issue. In the same issue appeared Morison's anonymous article, 'Black Letter: its history and current use'.

81. The Monotype Corporation: broadsheet specimen: 'Sachsenwald Gothic'
     (*Lent by the Monotype Corporation*)

EHRHARDT

82. **'Leipzig as a centre of type-founding',**
    in 'Signature', no. 11, March 1939,
    pp. 1–14

In this study of the late-seventeenth-century typefounders of Leipzig Morison observed that the narrowness and economy in space of Fraktur types had affected the design of those roman faces which local typefounders had gradually added to their stock, as the Leipzig book trade grew in importance. Letters attributed to the Dutch typefounder Anton Janson who worked in Leipzig were among those notable for their condensed but legible appearance. Morison particularly admired a series of such founts which had been displayed in a type specimen issued *c.* 1720 by the Ehrhardt foundry. Some of the original Ehrhardt matrices survived at the Stempel foundry, who had bought them in 1919, and from which they made and sold types under the name of Janson.

In 1937 permission was given for the issue of a version of Janson for Linotype casting; Morison secured the issue of a Monotype version in 1938 under the name of Ehrhardt. Further research by Harry Carter and G. Buday revealed that the designer of the parent types was not Janson, but Nicholas Kis, a Hungarian. (See H. Carter and G. Buday, 'Nicholas Kis and the Janson types', in *Gutenberg Jahrbuch*, 1957, pp. 207–12.)

SPECTRUM

Spectrum is the last of the three Monotype text faces designed by Van Krimpen. Spectrum was originally commissioned in 1939 as a Bible type and general book face, by the publishing house Het Spectrum of Utrecht, to be the firm's private property. The lower case was to be narrow, larger in x-height and bolder than is usual in a book face. The Monotype Corporation were asked to undertake the cutting of Spectrum, but at the end of the Second World War they were unwilling to proceed with an exclusive type at the expense of other business. The first sight of Van Krimpen's design reached Morison in smoke-proofs brought back by John Dreyfus on army leave in 1945. Eventually rights in the use of Spectrum were taken over by Enschedé; in 1950 Enschedé and Monotype agreed to produce it as another joint series which reached the trade in 1955.

DANTE

Giovanni Mardersteig designed Dante for his own private use at the Officina Bodoni; it was cut for him by Charles Malin and first used in an edition of Boccaccio, *Trattatello in laude di Dante*, 1954. As the new face appeared suitable for general book work, as well as for the printing of the limited editions for which it was designed, Morison was quick to recommend that permission be sought to cut a Monotype version. A range of sizes was issued between 1957 and 1959, developed from the original 10- and 12-point sizes.

In 1917 Bruce Rogers, then typographical adviser to the Cambridge University Press, submitted to the Syndics a report on improvements which were needed, in the course of which he pointed out the need for a wider range of good type faces. Until the suppliers of type and matrices had succeeded in issuing some acceptable new faces, Rogers's recommendations in this respect could obviously not be implemented; but with Morison's Monotype programme under way, and with the appointment as University Printer of Morison's friend and former colleague Walter Lewis in 1923, Cambridge printing entered a most distinguished period. Morison's direct connexion with the Cambridge University Press started during the first two years of Lewis's appointment when Morison often visited him to discuss, among other things, the first of his own works to be printed at Cambridge, *Four centuries of fine printing*. Lewis suggested to S. C. Roberts, Secretary to the Syndics, the appointment of Morison as typographical adviser to the Cambridge University Press, which was made on 1 January 1925. Morison continued to advise the Press until his death, except for the short period when he was editor of *The Times Literary Supplement*, and could not be associated with a publishing house.

83. 'Four centuries of fine printing.'
    Upwards of six hundred examples of
    the work of the presses established
    during the years 1500 to 1914. With an
    introductory text and indexes. Ernest
    Benn Limited: London, 1924. Letter-
    press printed at the University Press,
    Cambridge

Morison's first large folio is the most impressive and influential book he wrote in the 1920s.

In spite of the '1500' on the title page the first 16 plates illustrate books printed between 1470 and 1495. 'By a not easily justifiable device all consideration of typography in black-letter is excluded, the author then having no accurate knowledge of the subject.' The text of this book is the first showing of Monotype Poliphilus, set in the 16-point size.

F. G. Nobbs, the composing-room overseer at the Cambridge University Press, concocted a border of lower-case Blado 'g's for the title-page.

84. 'Modern fine printing.' An exhibit of
    printing issued in England, the United
    States of America, France, Germany,
    Italy, Switzerland, Czecho-Slovakia,
    Holland and Sweden during the
    twentieth century, and with few
    exceptions since the outbreak of the
    war. London: Ernest Benn Limited,
    1925

Modern fine printing did a great deal to introduce fine printing done abroad to British readers. 'This was originally designed and, in fact, collected by S. M. to form the concluding part of *Four centuries of fine printing* [83]. The amputation and separate publication was the decision of the publishers, in perhaps not quite the "right spirit" alluded to in "A right spirit in publishing"; though certainly the costs of both exceeded the estimates!' Morison had praised his publishers in his article 'A right spirit in publishing' (*Penrose's Annual*, no. 26, 1924), not only for their typography but for their scrupulous editorial methods.

The letterpress of the English and German editions was printed at the Cambridge University Press in Poliphilus, and the text of the French edition at the Pelican Press in Imprint.

85. 'German incunabula in the British Museum.' One hundred & fifty-two facsimile plates of fine book-pages from the presses of Germany, German-Switzerland and Austria-Hungary printed in the fifteenth century in Gothic letter and derived founts. With an introduction by Stanley Morison. London: Victor Gollancz Limited, 1928. (Printed by the Cambridge University Press.)
— Impression of the binding block designed by David Jones

(*Lent by Douglas Cleverdon Esq.*)

Morison later admitted that at the time he hardly understood that no useful appreciation of gothic typography was possible unless preceded by an adequate analysis of gothic calligraphy. His book was, however, 'the first attempt in English to go beyond identification and measurement, to the classification of "gothic". It leaves unresolved the problem of the supersession of "carolingian" by "gothic". This matter was not treated until *"Black-letter" text*, 1942' [103].

The block on the upper cover with its 'Sed libera nos a malo' device was designed by David Jones.

The frontispiece reproduces a wood engraving from the *Missale Constantiense*; Basel, Peter Kollicker, 1485.

86. 'A tally of types cut for machine composition and introduced at the University Press, Cambridge, 1922–1932.' Cambridge, privately printed, 1953

The Cambridge University Printer's Christmas book for 1953 is a vital source-book for Morison's work. The book contains a preface and postscript by Brooke Crutchley, the present University Printer, and wood engravings by Reynolds Stone, but consists mainly of Morison's own notes on those types in the Monotype programme which had been used at the Cambridge University Press. Each chapter is set in the type face it describes.

87. Poster: Cambridge University Press, 1521–1938
(*Lent by the University Printing House, Cambridge*)
This is one of several posters designed by Morison for the Cambridge University Press.

88. Photograph of Walter Lewis taken during the 1930s

89. Pencil note from Morison to Frank Gordon Nobbs, composing-room overseer at the Cambridge University Press
(*Lent by the University Printing House, Cambridge*)
Morison found to his lasting satisfaction that the standards of craftsmanship at the Cambridge University Press were already high. Walter Lewis, as exacting a judge of presswork as Morison was of composition, took endless pains to obtain a strong impression and to eliminate poor register or bad alignment, thus creating at Cambridge the conditions necessary for the successful realization of Morison's designs.

Morison was also particularly fortunate to find in the composing-room overseer, F. G. Nobbs, someone who was in sympathy with his ideas.

90. The Holy Bible. Cambridge, at the University Press, 1936

The design of the Pitt Brevier Bible, issued originally at the modest price of half-a-crown, in its combination of clarity with economy shows considerable skill and ingenuity.

The basic requirement of the text to be printed was, in fact, that the volume should sell for 2s. 6d. First the Printer worked out how many sheets he could afford to machine within this price-limit; next Morison established the maximum area upon the sheet which could actually carry text, and then designed the Times Semi-Bold version of Times New Roman to accommodate the text within these limits.

91. University of Cambridge: Honorary Degrees, 8 June 1950. The Orator's speech in presenting Morison to the Vice-Chancellor
(Lent by John Dreyfus Esq.)

92. Photograph of Morison in procession with the Revd Edmund Fellowes after receiving an honorary doctorate of letters
(Lent by the University Printing House, Cambridge)
In 1950 Sir Sydney Roberts, formerly Secretary of the Syndics of the University Press, became Vice-Chancellor of the University and had the satisfaction of putting Morison's name forward for an honorary doctorate, and of conferring upon him the degree of Litt.D. *honoris causa*.

Morison also received honorary degrees from the Universities of Birmingham, of Chatham, New Brunswick, and of Marquette, Wisconsin, and honorary fellowships of more than half a dozen learned societies. He refused three offers of a knighthood.

93. 'On learned presses.' A paper given to the Double Crown Club on the occasion of its 130th dinner held in King's College, Cambridge, on June 23rd 1955
(Lent by John Carter Esq.)
Morison's last Double Crown Club paper was printed at the University Press, Cambridge, and the last recto carries the following note by the University Printer: 'It is the business of a Learned Press to protect authors from the consequences of their own shortcomings; and so in view of the closeness of the time and of S.M.'s well known proclivity for rewriting his works in proof, we took the precaution of not sending him a proof of this paper. It has thus been possible to distribute copies on the occasion for which it was designed...' Morison's comment was: 'Ah, some misprints, owing to my not being permitted to correct proofs.'

The hero of Morison's paper was Marcello Cervini, Prefect of the Vatican Library, promoter of Greek studies and printing, virtual founder of the learned press at the Vatican, and, as Marcellus II, Pope in 1555.

94. Morison's sketch layout made in 1926 for Fournier-le-jeune's 'Traité historique et critique sur l'origine et les progrès des caractères de fonte pour l'impression de la musique, 1765'.
Edited in type facsimile with an introduction & appendices by Paul Beaujon. [Unpublished.] Title page and p. 1
(Lent by Nicolas Barker Esq.)
Beatrice Warde's type-facsimile edition of Fournier-le-jeune's last work remained unpublished. Galleys were printed, set in Barbou, at the Cambridge University Press, and Morison provided this complete sketch layout.

CALLIGRAPHY: HISTORY OF LETTER-FORMS

Morison's study of early printing led him to investigate the handwriting of the fifteenth and sixteenth centuries, the patterns on which the first type faces were modelled. His first book on calligraphy was on Ludovico degli Arrighi [52], a man equally important as a calligrapher, writing master and printer in types based on the chancery cursive hand. Sometimes in cooperation with other scholars, Morison published editions and facsimiles of writing-books and surveys of the history of letter-forms, of which a selection only can be shown here.

95. Specimen of calligraphy by Rudolf Koch, presented by him to Morison, 4 November 1922

96. Letter of thanks from Morison to Koch, 5 November 1922
   (*Lent by Berthold Wolpe Esq.*)
Rudolf Koch (1876–1934), calligrapher and typographer, enjoyed in Germany a reputation equal to Eric Gill's in England. He was a designer for the Klingspor type foundry at Offenbach am Main and taught calligraphy in the School of Arts and Crafts in that town, where Morison visited him. Koch's letters in writing and type design drew their inspiration from the traditional German gothic forms.

97. Letter from Edward Johnston to Morison, dated Ditchling, 12 December 1923   (*Lent by Nicolas Barker Esq.*)

98. 'Andres Brun, calligrapher of Saragossa: Some account of his life and work, by Henry Thomas and Stanley Morison. With a facsimile in collotype of the surviving text and plates of his two writing books, 1583 and 1612.' Paris: The Pegasus Press, 1929
— Prospectus
(*Lent by the Curators of the Bodleian Library*)
Andres Brun, a teacher of calligraphy, published two treatises on handwriting, for which he himself cut the woodblocks giving examples. Morison's friend Thomas was a distinguished scholar in the field of Spanish literature and bibliography.

The text, hand-set in Janson type, was printed upon the hand-press of the Officina Bodoni, Verona, November 1928, and published by John Holroyd Reece's Pegasus Press, the publishers of a number of Morison's limited editions.

99. (a) 'Fra Luca de Pacioli of Borgo San Sepolcro.' The Grolier Club: New York, 1933.
— (b) Prospectus
(*Lent by the Curators of the Bodleian Library*)
Fra Luca de Pacioli, Franciscan friar and mathematician, is best known for his *Summa de arithmetica*, 1494, containing an early description of double-entry book-keeping. The present work, however, as Morison explains, describes those sections of Pacioli's *De divina proportione*, 1509, which comprise diagrams of the true shapes and proportions of classical Roman letters, and provide some discussion of lettering in the interests of architects and their stone-cutters. The alphabet in Morison's Grolier Club volume is reproduced in the size of the original (from a copy lent by Philip Hofer who also provided the bibliographical notes) and printed with a translation of the friar's instructions. 'The majesty of the engraved letters', wrote Morison in his Preface, 'amply justified full-size reproduction.' Bruce Rogers, designer of the Grolier Club editions of the alphabets of Dürer and Geofroy Tory, was in Morison's words 'responsible for the typistry (as he perversely calls it) of the present volume'. This book, on which three of the most eminent figures of modern printing, Rogers, Lewis and Morison, collaborated, was printed in Monotype Centaur at the Cambridge University Press.

— (c) Bound set of page proofs with corrections and autograph notes by Morison and Bruce Rogers
(*Lent by Ben Grauer Esq.*)
Morison's corrections and annotations are in both ink and pencil; the smaller pencil notes are in Rogers's hand.

A

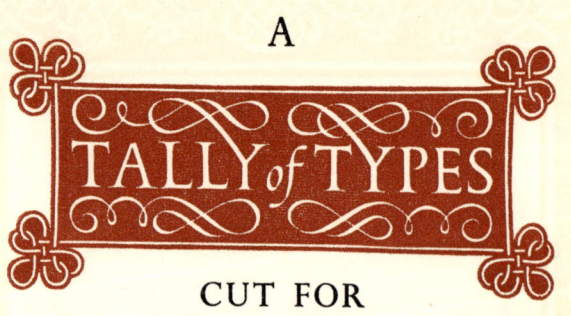

TALLY *of* TYPES

CUT FOR
MACHINE COMPOSITION
AND
INTRODUCED AT
THE UNIVERSITY PRESS
CAMBRIDGE

1922–1932

CAMBRIDGE
PRIVATELY PRINTED
1953

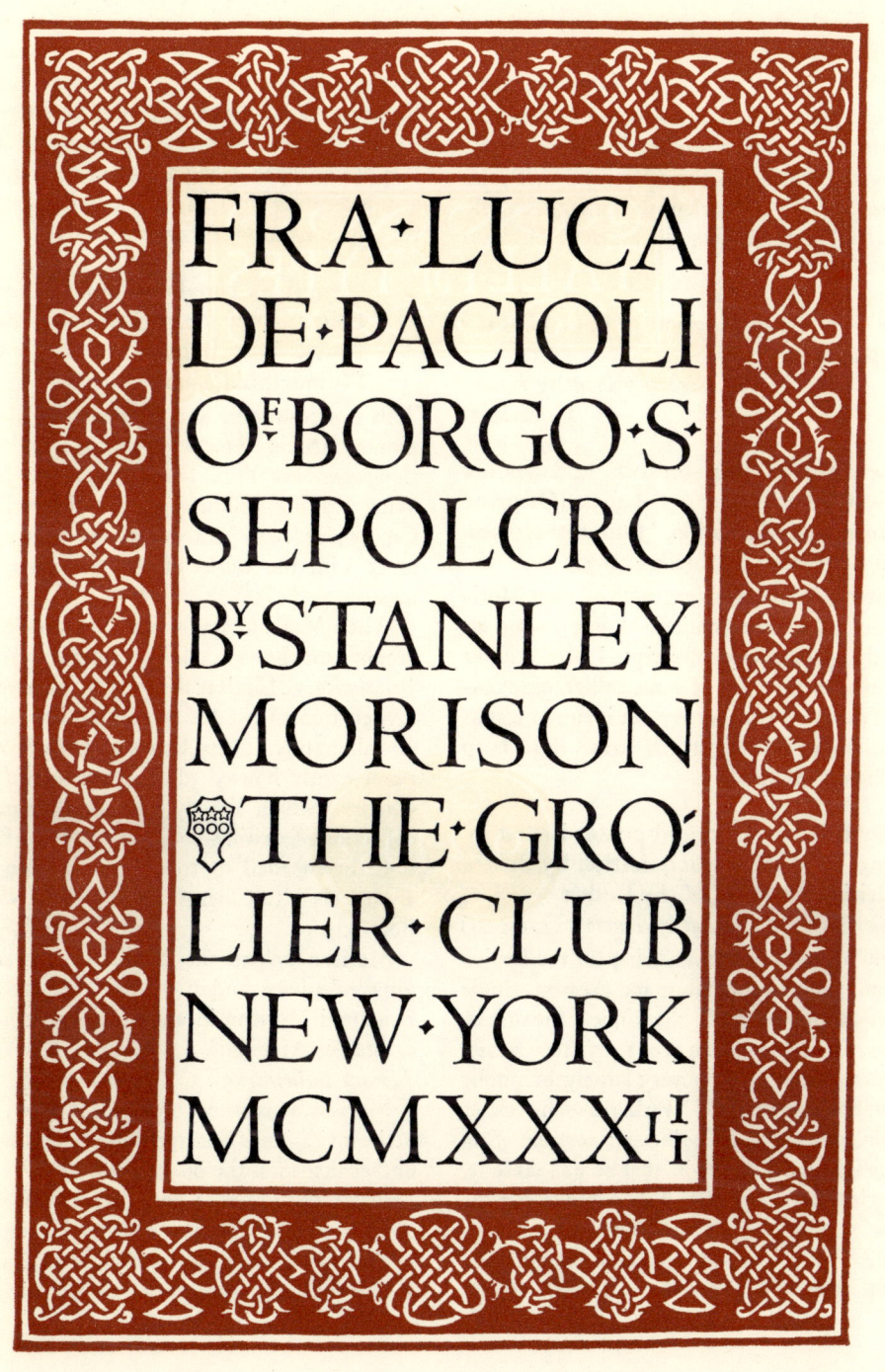

FRA · LUCA
DE · PACIOLI
OF BORGO · S ·
SEPOLCRO
BY STANLEY
MORISON
THE · GRO-
LIER · CLUB
NEW · YORK
MCMXXXII

99a   [12½ × 8¼ in.]

— (d) **Single sheet of proof (p. 39) with a pencil note by Walter Lewis**
(*Lent by Ronald Mansbridge Esq.*)

Lewis compares two pages proofed in different inks, which he refers to by the letters on them. Lewis wrote: 'The F is the right ink – matt, the C having varnish and driers did not satisfy BR [i.e. Rogers]; certainly you get a denser black on the F.'

— (e) **Note from Morison to F. G. Nobbs, dated 25. 5. 33**
(*Lent by the University Printing House, Cambridge*)

100. Letter from Morison to E. E. Reynolds on handwriting, 5 April 1932. (Offprint from E. E. Reynolds, 'Junior exercises in English'. Cambridge, 1932)

This letter is itself a good example of what Morison required in handwriting. 'I like to see an obviously speedy piece of script. I hate a letter which exhales the scent of some calligraphic cosmetic. Give me a true cursive, let it run as fast as one can make it and at the same time keep it sufficiently regular.'

101. London Underground poster issued in 1934 to mark the acquisition by the British Museum of the Codex Sinaiticus (*Lent by London Transport*)

Morison played a part in securing for the British Museum what is probably its greatest single acquisition this century, the Codex Sinaiticus, sold to the Museum in 1933 by the Soviet Government and paid for very largely by public subscription. Maurice L. Ettinghausen relates in *Rare books and royal collectors: memoirs of an antiquarian book-seller*, 1966, that he was asked by the Soviet Government to find a buyer for the famous fourth-century Biblical manuscript. Ettinghausen discussed possible purchasers with Morison, and it was Morison who acted as intermediary with Sir Frederic Kenyon, recently retired director of the British Museum and president of the Friends of the National Libraries. So great was the interest in the purchase of the Codex that the London Underground printed this poster reproducing a page of the manuscript and indicating (in Gill Sans letters) the nearest tube stations to the Museum.

102. 'American copybooks: an outline of their history from Colonial to modern times.' Wm. F. Fell Co., Printers: Philadelphia, 1951

This is a re-writing and expansion of Morison's pioneer article 'American penmanship' in *The Colophon*, New York, Part 17, 1934. As John M. Wing Visiting Fellow at the Newberry Library, Chicago, in 1949 Morison renewed his acquaintance with the works of the American writing masters.

When Morison was writing his article 'Calligraphy' for the 14th edition of the *Encyclopaedia Britannica*, C. Lindsay Ricketts of Wilmette, Wis., invited him to use his writing-books and books on calligraphy. These books were from 1941 on permanently housed in the Newberry Library, Chicago, which already possessed a remarkable collection of writing-books in the Wing Foundation. From 1948 to 1962 Morison paid almost annual visits to Chicago, initially as a Newberry Fellow.

Morison helped the Newberry Library with gifts and advice, and in October 1960 the Library honoured Morison in an exhibition 'The Work of Stanley Morison', described in *The Newberry Library Bulletin*, vol. 5, August 1960, pp. 159–72.

Morison's visits to Chicago continued: in 1961 at the invitation of Senator William Benton, owner and chairman of the board of directors of the *Encyclopaedia Britannica*, he became a member of the *Encyclopaedia Britannica* Board of Editors. Morison's thirst for information made him an assiduous reader and collector of encyclopaedias; he had

'BLACK-LETTER' TEXT

BY S.M.

ENGLISH BRASS LETTERED IN CONDENSED *TEXTUS QUADRATUS*

Engraved *circa* 1405 for the Church of Holme-by-the-Sea, Norfolk. (Monumental Brass Society's Portfolio, vol. III, 4)

Herry Notingham & hys wyffe lyne here | that maden this Churche stepull & quere | two vestmentz & bellez they made also | crist [t]hem save therfore ffro wo | ande to bringe [t]her saules to blis of heven | sayth pater & ave with mylde steven

CAMBRIDGE: PRINTED AT THE UNIVERSITY PRESS

1942

laid down the basic design of the 1950 edition of
Chambers' Encyclopedia

103. ' "Black-letter" text.' Cambridge,
     printed at the University Press, 1942
— Proofs corrected by Morison
                    (*Lent by Nicolas Barker Esq.*)

Morison sought 'to discover as precisely as possible why this open, round roman [the Carolingian
minuscule] was transformed into the pointed,
narrow "gothic", and what was gained by the
change'.

In the preface Morison describes the great air-
raid of 9–10 May 1941, which destroyed Morison's
rooms at 10 Cambridge Gate and most of his
papers and books. In the same raid the typescript
of selected calligraphical and typographical studies
ready for publication by Harvard University
Press was destroyed by a direct hit on the Monotype Corporation's premises. Morison was able
to rescue from the fire at Cambridge Gate this
paper and the materials for 'Early humanistic
script and the first roman type', which was published in *The Library*, vol. 24, June–September
1943.

104. 'Notes on the development of Latin
     script from early to modern times.'
     Cambridge, printed at the
     University Press, 1959
                    (*Lent by John Carter Esq.*)

These *Notes on the development of Latin script*
incorporate a revised and expanded version of
Latin script since the Renaissance, 1938, and take
in passages from other articles by Morison, in
particular from 'Early humanistic script and the
first roman type'.

At least as early as 1929 Morison had con-
ceived the idea of writing a comprehensive history
of letter-forms. He abandoned this project after
the loss of his books and papers during the Blitz
but *Notes on the development of Latin script* and
'*Black-letter*' *text* were completed and printed.

105. 'Aspects of authority and freedom in
     relation to Graeco-Latin script, in-
     scription and type, sixth century B.C.
     to twentieth century A.D.' The Lyell
     lectures. Delivered at Oxford, May
     1957. [Privately printed for Morison
     by The Times Publishing Co. Ltd.
     and by the Cambridge University
     Press.] With a set of Morison's manu-
     script notes for his exordium to the
     first lecture   (*Lent by John Carter Esq.*)

Morison's assignment to deliver the Lyell lectures
at the University of Oxford gave him the opportunity of consolidating and connecting his researches in the fields of epigraphy, palaeography
and typography, and to place them in a wider
historical context. Almost from the outset of his
career Morison had pondered deeply on the evolution of letter-forms, and his political and religious reading had later led him to trace the
influence of spiritual and political power on these
changes in style.

As with most of Morison's post-war lectures a
printed text (differing widely from the lecture as
delivered) was prepared for the purpose of
provoking corrections and distributed among his
audience.

The lectures are to be published later this year,
under the title of *Politics and Script*, by the
Oxford University Press.

106. Photograph showing (from left to
     right) Morison, John Carter and E. A.
     Lowe and taken by Alan Pryce-Jones
     at Princeton, N.J., 1962
                    (*Lent by John Carter Esq.*

Morison's friendship with E. A. Lowe, the palaeo-
grapher, went back to the article 'Calligraphy'
which Morison wrote for the 14th edition of the
Encyclopaedia Britannica in 1928, and which he
submitted to Lowe for comment. The article,
which Lowe warmly commended, has not been
superseded.

＊ MEETING ¶ FEDERATION OF MASTER PRINTERS

ANNUAL

BLACKPOOL

PUBLICITY AND
SELLING CONGRESS

on Monday, 21st May, 1928

at the Imperial Hydro Hotel

at 2.30 p.m.

A wide range of printers' flowers is now available and taken for granted; Morison and Meynell in a number of articles and designs did much to dispel apathy and ignorance concerning this minor but attractive embellishment of printing.

107. **Francis Meynell and Stanley Morison: 'Printers' flowers and arabesques', in 'The Fleuron', 1, 1923, pp. 1–43**

This article, the first general study of printers' flowers (soon followed by the Monotype revival of a series of flowers), marks the culmination of Morison's reintroduction of 'colour' into printing. Thereafter he concentrated on logical order [37].

In his later work Morison rarely used flowers such as those described here.

108. **The Monotype Corporation: specimen broadsheet: new series of Monotype decorations cast from 18- and 24-point matrices [1923]**
(Lent by the Monotype Corporation)

109. **'On the typographical ornaments of Granjon, Fournier and Weiss', in 'E. R. Weiss: zum fünfzigsten Geburtstage, 12 Oktober 1925'. Leipzig: Insel-Verlag, 1926. (Photograph)**

'An historical and practical dissertation on baroque, rococo and neo-rococo fleurons.'

This illustration reproduces the title-page of La Fontaine's *The old maid's marriage*, translated by Edward Marsh, 'presented as a specimen of type based on the design of Pierre-Simon Fournier (le jeune)...by Stanley Morison'.

110. **'Venice and the arabesque ornament.' For the Oxford University Bibliophiles, November 17, 1955**
(Lent by John Carter Esq.)

This address to an undergraduate group is an inquiry into the process by which a form of ornament used architecturally, in textiles and in other artefacts in the Near East became part of the equipment of printers and binders in Western Europe.

111. **'Splendour of ornament.' By Stanley Morison. Specimens selected from the 'Essempio di recammi', the first Italian manual of decoration, Venice 1524, by Giovanni Antonio Tagliente. His life and literary remains by Esther Potter. Preface by Berthold Wolpe. Lion and Unicorn Press: London, 1968**

The *Essempio di recammi* is a treatise by the Italian sixteenth-century calligrapher Giovanni Antonio Tagliente on embroidered, sewn and woven ornament, illustrated by fine patterns which Morison wished to bring to the notice of contemporary students. Morison had for long admired, collected and used Tagliente's writing-books.

Morison adduces his reasons for the modern study and practice of ornament, and gives a brief outline of the bibliography of the *Essempio* and later similar pattern-books. In the original editions the patterns were badly compromised by careless press-work on cheap, thin paper; and so photographs were retouched for the preparation of the blocks and some were redrawn by Victor Lardent for *Splendour of ornament*.

112. Eleven book jackets, designed by Morison for Victor Gollancz Ltd.

(Lent by John Dreyfus Esq.)

Morison acted at various times as typographical adviser to a number of publishers and printers: Doubleday (in New York), Lund Humphries, Heinemann and Ernest Benn. In 1927 Victor Gollancz left Ernest Benn to set up his own publishing business in London, of which Morison was one of the directors from 1928 to 1938. In 1929 he introduced simple standard formats for books (one for politics, another for fiction), and strident book jackets on yellow paper, packed with varied sizes and weights of block lettering and other display faces, fists and quotation marks. Customers – potential readers – had first to be compelled to look at a jacket and then induced to start reading at once. This, Morison maintained, needed typographical audacity. He began a discussion of the book's contents on the front of its bright yellow jacket in order to make the reader turn to the flap and open the book. He made a clear distinction between the unobtrusive typography suitable for books, and the typography of publicity, which must attract attention. The salesmen preferred picture jackets, but Morison's designs were nevertheless very successful, and Gollancz jackets continued in his style.

FEDERATION OF MASTER PRINTERS' CONGRESS, 1928

113. Federation of Master Printers. Publicity and Selling Congress. Programme 1928. An interim proof of Gill sans-serif titling

114. 'The 2 kinds of effectiveness'

115. 'Robbing the printer', in the Federation of Master Printers 'Members' Circular', June 1928, pp. 182–6   *(Lent by John Dreyfus Esq.)*

In 1928 Morison was invited to address the Publicity and Selling Committee of the Federation of Master Printers at their annual congress at Blackpool. He took the opportunity to introduce in the programme he designed for the meeting a first showing of Gill Sans, intended as an example of a lucid and attention-holding piece of display. The programme, circulated before the meeting, provoked violent criticism on account of its eccentric layout and 'Gollancz-style' yellow cover. To this Morison made a preliminary counter-attack in a leaflet *The 2 kinds of effectiveness* which his audience found waiting for them on their seats. In his address, 'Robbing the printer', Morison maintained that jobbing printers, by their attachment to the conventions of book printing, were being 'robbed' of the chance to design publicity and display material (where novelty and effectiveness are essential) by middle men.

'People in publishing and publicity have lost faith in the printer. They do not believe that he has either intelligence enough or resourcefulness enough, or brains, type or anything of value to them', except machines. To reverse this, Morison argued, 'more types will be necessary, more inventiveness, more interest in typography... Advertising men have no more brains than printers, but they use them'.

The Times in the issue of 3 October 1932 adopted a complete new 'dress' or layout, based on Times New Roman, the type face Morison designed for this purpose [77]. This radical change was the result of Morison's outspoken criticisms of the paper's typography, provoked by *The Times* management's offer to set and print a Monotype Corporation advertisement in *The Times* Printing Supplement of 29 October 1929. Morison in fact contributed an article (anonymous) to this supplement, 'Newspaper types: a study of *The Times*', in which his concluding remarks were: 'The question of an ideal type is, indeed, one of the greatest difficulty, complexity and risk for any newspaper, and whatever the final result of recently conducted experiments, the type of this present Printing Number remains that of its predecessor of 17 years ago' [3]. Morison was by this time typographical adviser to *The Times*, as well as to the Cambridge University Press and the Monotype Corporation.

116. 'Memorandum on a proposal to reform the typography of "The Times", 1930.' Printed at the office of 'The Times', 21 November 1930

Morison wrote this 34-page memorandum (printed in an edition of 25 copies) for the guidance of the committee appointed to consider the alteration of the paper's type.

The memorandum began with a résumé of the history of letter-forms and a reminder of *The Times*'s character and readership, and went on to investigate newspaper type in particular, and how this could be improved. The Medical Research Council's findings in their '*Report on the legibility of print*', 1926, are cited in support of a new type face for *The Times*. Morison's object was 'by articulating the problem of a new type with relevant details of past and present practice, to assist the committee towards the adoption of a fount which shall be English in its basic tradition, new, though free from conscious archaism or conscious art, losing no scintilla of that "legibility" which rests on fundamental ocular laws, or that "readability" which rests upon age-long customs of the eye'.

117. 'Supplement to the memorandum on a proposal to revise the typography of "The Times".' Printed at the office of 'The Times', 12 June 1931

The proposals in Morison's first memorandum were accepted by the committee, but his most revolutionary suggestion, the replacement of the eighteenth-century black-letter title-piece by one in roman letters (to match the roman type of the text), required further justification. These arguments are to be found in this *Supplement*, together with suggestions for redrawing the Royal Arms – the paper's device appearing on the title-piece without patent or warrant. John Walter, the first proprietor of the paper, bought the Printing House (from which Printing House Square is named) in 1784, and this building bore the Royal Arms on its pediment which the King's Printers (the former occupants of the building) had displayed in virtue of their patent. From the beginning the proprietors of *The Times* had used these arms in the title-piece of the newspaper which they printed in this Printing House.

Morison proposed retaining the 'clock device', which appears daily in close proximity to the leading article, 'from every point of view, traditional and actual, the aptest flag for *The Times* to keep flying at its masthead'.

Although the black-letter title-piece was regarded by some of the owners and management of *The Times* as their trademark and part of the paper's character, Morison in advocating a roman title-piece was only urging a return to original practice: when *The Daily Universal Register* in 1788 became *The Times* the heading was roman.

118. 'The typography of "The Times" illustrated in upwards of forty plates from originals between January 1, 1785, and June 16, 1930.' Printing House Square, 1930

(Lent by Times Newspapers Ltd.)

So that the chief proprietor of *The Times*, Major the Hon. J. J. Astor (later Lord Astor of Hever), would have an idea of the historical background against which Morison's proposals for his paper were to be seen, Morison prepared this large folio in an edition of one copy which was presented to the chief proprietor by the staff of *The Times*. (There is, in fact, another copy which Morison retained for his own use, now in the Cambridge University Library.) The large format was required by the need to reproduce legibly full-page facsimiles of back numbers of *The Times*. The text and descriptions of the 42 collotype plates, though unsigned, were written by Morison, and keyboarded on one of the Monotype machines at Printing House Square for large composition, i.e. in 24-point Bembo, for which the matrices were specially cut.

119. 'The Times', Saturday, 1 October 1932

This was the last issue of *The Times* to appear in the old typography, and the last appearance of the gothic title-piece.

Morison's typographical reform meant a complete re-styling of *The Times*'s outward appearance: a clear and logical layout, so that features could be easily found; the gradation of headings; and the rearrangement of the leader page. It is fair to say that Morison's 'new look' made *The Times* the most handsome and best-designed English newspaper.

120. 'The Times', Monday, 3 October 1932

By coincidence the introduction of the new type took place on the 100th anniversary of the death of Friedrich Koenig, who with Andreas Bauer had printed *The Times* by steam in 1814 on the first power press to be made workable. This first issue in the new 'dress' – the format remained unchanged – triumphantly bears out Morison's fundamental argument for the design of Times New Roman:

'The primary editorial requirement is space, and at the best of times every newspaper suffers from a shortage of it, daily newspapers most of all – and *The Times* as a "national register" as well as a newspaper, more than all others. It had been made clear in the early stage of the inquiry that no new design could be considered satisfactory that failed to bring in at least as many characters in an equivalent space as that taken by the design it was intended to supersede.'

The black-letter title-piece was, of course, replaced; and the Royal Arms were a re-engraving of the block used in 1792, although Morison had recommended that of 1788. In 1953 the title-piece was redesigned by Reynolds Stone to Morison's specification.

121. 'Printing "The Times": a record of the changes introduced in the issue of 3 October 1932.' Printing House Square, 1932 *(Lent by John Carter Esq.)*

Prepared as part of the detailed publicity programme for the changes, *Printing 'The Times': a record of the changes* gives a short non-technical account (with six pages of type specimens) of a revision 'unique in the history of newspapers; doubly so, since the forms and sizes of all the new types were specified, originated and designed exclusively by Printing House Square'.

122. 'Printing "The Times" since 1785. Some account of the means of production and changes of dress of the newspaper, illustrated with upwards of fifty facsimiles of pages and many line engravings &c.' London: Printing House Square, 1953

This large folio was planned, edited and for the most part written by Morison, very largely to meet the criticism that *The history of 'The Times'* gave no technical account of the production of the paper. This information was now provided in abundance, with full-sized illustrations of *The Times* from 1785 to date. The text was based on *The typography of 'The Times'* [118]; the Chiswick Press was able to provide the original collotype plates.

123. 'The History of "The Times".' London: written, printed and published at the office of 'The Times', 1935–52

The idea of a history of *The Times* grew out of the work of G. E. Buckle, editor from 1884 to 1912. Morison's Sandars Lectures suggested that Morison might be the man to set the history moving and in 1934 he wrote his first instalment, on the period covered by the editorship of Thomas Barnes. Morison was eventually given facilities to edit and virtually to write *The History of 'The Times'* which appeared in 4 volumes between 1935 and 1952: vol. 1 was published on 1 January 1935, on the occasion of the paper's 150th anniversary, vol. 2 on 13 February 1939, vol. 3 on 2 December 1948 and vol. 4 on 23 April 1952. The *History* was published both in trade and *de luxe* editions, the latter separately set and spectacularly illustrated not only with 'zincos' but with wood engravings, gravure and collotype.

The preface in vol. 1 stated that the book was intended to be 'the history of *The Times*, not of contemporary politics as seen from Printing House Square'. Morison did not in fact allow himself to be restricted by this directive, and saw to it that the *History* took in the effect of the paper on politics, of politics on *The Times*, and of both upon public opinion. Morison's scholarship is matched by his candour. He rediscovered Barnes, the editor under whom *The Times* attained a unique influence. Morison's unvarnished picture of Northcliffe showed him as an equal power in the twentieth century. The relationship Morison established during his researches with the chief proprietor and board of directors (some information on policy could come only from them) led to his being consulted on matters other than typography and history.

124. Bill posters for the issues of 'The Times Literary Supplement' of 22 February 1936 and 14 May 1938, designed by Morison

(Lent by Arthur Crook Esq.)

During the late 1930s Morison had become critical of the way *The Times Literary Supplement* was run, which eventually led to his appointment as editor, from 1945 to 1948. With Morison as editor, *The Times Literary Supplement* abandoned insularity; American and foreign books were extensively reviewed; obituaries and crossword puzzles were dropped; and a major front-page article reinstated; Morison employed well-known scholars to write for the *Supplement* and maintained a new level of seriousness and purpose. The *TLS* increased its circulation and began to achieve an international standing.

125. Four posters designed by Morison for 'The Times', 1954

These Quad Royal posters, printed in two or more colours, were displayed on London Underground stations.

126. 'John Bell, 1745–1831, Bookseller, Printer, Publisher, Typefounder, Journalist, etc.' Printed for the author at the University Press, Cambridge, 1930

After the production of Monotype Bell had been put in hand Walter Lewis, the Cambridge University Printer, at Morison's suggestion, instructed him to write a brief description of Bell's type, to be elegantly produced and distributed to his clients as a Christmas book. 'A somewhat inordinate zeal extended the text beyond the sixteen pages of my commission', wrote Morison, who found Bell himself to be an engaging character, 'a pugnacious, benevolent, careless bohemian who became the most resourceful and inventive bookseller of his generation, a fine printer, a notable journalist and the unacknowledged pioneer of modern type-design in England.' He was the first English printer to discard the long 's'. When this study developed into a book of nearly 200 pages with 18 plates, the plan to issue it as a Printer's Christmas book was abandoned.

The book was not set in Monotype Bell, but handset in types specially cast from Bell's original matrices. The full yet well-ordered title-page, the decorative headpieces and rules are graceful allusions to Bell's own practice.

The First Editions Club supported Morison's publishing venture with an exhibition in 1931 and by taking 100 copies for its members.

127. 'Captain Edward Topham, Mrs Mary Wells, The Keep-the-Line Club, &c., &c.', in 'The Colophon', New York, part 6, 1931. Printed at the Cambridge University Press

(Lent by John Dreyfus Esq.)

128. 'Edward Topham, 1751–1820. Eton and Trin. Coll. Camb., Author of "The Fool" and other farces, Conductor of "The World and Fashionable Advertiser"' [etc.]. Cambridge, printed by W. Lewis at the University Press for friends in the printing and publishing trades, New Year's Day, 1933

In 1787 Captain Edward Topham and John Bell founded *The World and Fashionable Advertiser*, which Topham continued to edit and publish until 1794. The typography of his newspaper, which the layout of the *Colophon* version of Morison's essay reflects and even parodies, was both elegant and original. The same could be said of Topham himself: a dandy, playwright, captain, magistrate, satirist, fox-hunter, 'protector' of the actress Mrs Mary Wells, and a founding member of the 'Keep-the-Line' Club (each member of which was bound to regale the Club with a dozen bottles of claret every time he published anything). The portraits by Rowlandson were printed from copper and coloured by hand.

ICHABOD DAWKS AND HIS NEWS-LETTERS

Ichabod Dawks (1661–1731), the grandson of a bookseller and son of a printer, published and printed several newspapers: *The Philosophical Observer* (1695), *The Protestant Mercury* (1697) and, most notably, *Dawks's News-letter* (1699–1716). Dawks printed this last journal in his own script type, specially designed in 1696. Morison proposed John and Thomas Grover as the typefounders who cut the Dawks scriptorial face, which is a simplified and anglicized version of the Italian handwriting taught by such writing masters as Martin Billingsley.

129. The Memorandum book of Thomas and Ichabod Dawks

(*Department of Manuscripts. Add. ms. 42 101*)

Morison found in a bookshop the memorandum book of the Dawks family, lost since the eighteenth century, and presented it to the British Museum. It is a manuscript notebook on religious matters written by the Puritan Richard Wharfe, an heirloom afterwards used up by Thomas Dawks and his son Ichabod for family and business memoranda, in which are recorded on the fly-leaf the births, deaths and marriages of their family. The book was bound by a later owner and labelled 'Dawks Diary'.

130. 'Ichabod Dawks and his "News-letter", with an account of the Dawks family of booksellers and stationers, 1635–1731.' Cambridge, at the University Press, 1931

131. The Double Crown Club, March 20th 1930. Illustrations to a paper on Ichabod Dawks and his newsletters

(*Lent by the estate of the late Stanley Morison*)

Besides giving details concerning Thomas Dawks I, bookseller and later minister of St Michael's, Queenhithe, and of Thomas Dawks II, 'printer to His Majesty in the British language (i.e. Welsh)', this volume chronicles the career in printing of Ichabod Dawks and his establishment as a newspaper man. The facsimile of *Dawks's News-letter* of 3 August 1699 is a resetting in Dawks's script type cast by the firm of Stephenson, Blake to whom the original matrices had descended. The several headings used during the newspaper's life were recut. The reproductions included collotype facsimiles of issues of *The Philosophical Observer* and *The Protestant Mercury*, of a four-page manuscript newsletter, and of several pages from the Dawks family memorandum book. A folder of transcriptions and illustrations, which included these reproductions,

had been printed at Cambridge to accompany a paper Morison read to the Double Crown Club.

132. ' "The English newspaper". Some account of the physical development of journals printed in London between 1622 and the present day.' Cambridge, at the University Press, 1932

This extended version of the Sandars Lectures in Bibliography delivered by Morison in Cambridge in February 1932 is the standard history of the English newspaper.

Morison examined, not the content but the form of newspapers, from the earliest 'corantos' to the latest evening paper. He showed how the form has often been determined by the mechanical means of production. This was a new approach to the subject, illuminated by Morison's wide knowledge of printing and publishing techniques over the centuries. 'Newspapers', Morison pointed out, 'are the invention of the printer, and printing is absolutely essential to newspapers, as opposed to books.' The text is the first showing of Monotype Bell.

133. Title-pieces of newspapers before and after redesigning by Morison:

Daily Worker: 30 April and 1 May 1930
Reynolds News: 23 February and 1 March 1936
Daily Express: 18 July and 20 July 1942
Daily Herald: 23 September and 29 September 1944
Financial Times: 29 September and 1 October 1945

A feature of newspapers which Morison considered in need of improvement was the title-piece. We have seen how Morison waited until *The Times* was pretty well committed to a typographical reform before he proposed the substitution of a title-piece in roman letter for the 'Gothick' title-piece which many people thought traditional.

In 1930 he had cut a block for a bold sans-serif title-piece for the *Daily Worker*, which was introduced, appropriately enough, on 1 May. Although Morison was on close terms with a number of the original members of the British Communist Party, including Page Arnot and Walter Holmes of the *Daily Worker*, it is unlikely that either they (or Morison himself) seriously considered Morison's Catholicism and his known individualism a suitable basis for Party membership.

Morison was responsible for the design of one of the numerous *Daily Herald* title-pieces and title-pieces for the *Financial Times*, *Daily Express* (still in use) and *Reynolds News*.

MORISON AND LORD BEAVERBROOK

134. Letter from Morison to Lord Beaverbrook, dated Printing House Square, 14 May 1952

135. Note of thanks from Morison to Lord Beaverbrook, September 1952

136. Photograph of Morison looking at the grave of Karl Marx in Highgate Cemetery, 1952
    (*Lent by the Beaverbrook Library*)

In 1948 Morison and Beaverbrook met on board the *Queen Mary*; Morison was naturally interested to meet the newspaper-owner who had known Lord Northcliffe and anxious to learn more from the Lloyd George papers which Beaverbrook eventually bought. Beaverbrook, for his part, was interested to find out from Morison about Lord Northcliffe's ownership of *The Times*, and about such matters as *The Times* and the abdication of Edward VIII. Beaverbrook, an advocate of private enterprise and Empire free trade, was a royalist and a Presbyterian, while Morison was a socialist, a republican and a Catholic. The two men, despite their differences (and, to some extent, because of them), became friends.

Beaverbrook, in the course of two broadcasts given in May 1952, reviewed vol. 4 of *The History of 'The Times'* and found in it support for his view of the Abdication crisis. Beaverbrook began his television broadcast by interviewing the historian of *The Times*, shown looking at Karl Marx's grave. Morison's letter congratulating Beaverbrook on the broadcast jubilantly compares him with Northcliffe. The inscribed picture of Dom Pérignon's statue expresses thanks to Beaverbrook for copious draughts of Morison's favourite champagne.

137. 'At P.H.S. – The voice of the wicked Lord B——': engraving from a watercolour by Laurence Irving
(*Lent by the University Printing House, Cambridge*)
This caricature by a colleague of Morison's at *The Times* depicts Beaverbrook as Mephistopheles tempting the historian of *The Times*.

THE WISE FORGERIES

138. Letter from Morison to Graham Pollard, dated on board the Cunard RMS 'Berengaria', 31 January 1933
    (*Lent by Graham Pollard Esq.*)
Morison played a part in the discovery of the typographical evidence which helped the exposure of T. J. Wise's forgeries of first editions;

John Carter and Graham Pollard published their findings in July 1934 in *An Enquiry into the nature of certain nineteenth century pamphlets*. In the autumn of 1932 Pollard had asked Morison to examine the copy in the Pierpont Morgan Library (as there was no copy available in any public library in England) of the Reading '1847' edition of Elizabeth Barrett Browning's *Sonnets from the Portuguese*. Morison, *en route* to New York, wrote to Pollard: 'I think there is something in the 'f' and 'j' and '?' of that type which I wouldn't expect in those letters in 1847.' On his return journey he wrote again to Pollard about these letters, which were broken-backed and kernless – sorts evolved in order to prevent broken kerns occurring, especially during the distribution of type. Pollard then searched the type-specimens in the St Bride Printing Library for the earliest appearance of these kernless letters and found that they first occurred in Shanks & Co.'s specimen of 1883. Pollard then found the 'button-hook'

'f' and 'j' and the suspect '?' in another work printed by Richard Clay for T. J. Wise. From this and from other evidence, especially paper analysis, the forgery was proved. Morison had first made Pollard's acquaintance when arranging for the retailing of his *Calligraphic models of Ludovico degli Arrighi*. Pollard, among whose specialities as a bookseller were writing-books and early newspapers, showed Morison many of the examples later reproduced in *The English newspaper*. They dined together regularly in the 1930s and visited Whitstable every year at the beginning of the oyster season.

THE FELL TYPES

The Fell types of the University Press at Oxford are cast in matrices bequeathed to the University by John Fell (1625–86), Dean of Christ Church and Bishop of Oxford, an ardent promoter of good and learned printing.

The roman and italic types of Fell's gift came back into favour late in the nineteenth century, after long disuse, and have been seen in many fine editions from the University Press, which reserves them for its own use and casts them in its own typefoundry. They are the oldest type faces now in commercial use.

The origin of these type faces has, until lately, been a mystery. Horace Hart, Printer to the University (1883–1915), published in 1900 some correspondence of Fell's which showed that he bought matrices from Dutch typefounders in 1670 and 1672. Therefore it was assumed that the types named after him were made in Holland in the seventeenth century.

Morison's interest in the problem was first aroused by Gustav Mori's facsimile (published in 1920) of the Sabon-Berner typefounder's speci-

men sheet of 1592; this contained an italic attributed to the French punch-cutter Robert Granjon (d. 1589), which Morison recognized as one of the types bought by Bishop Fell. Morison recognized several more of the Fell romans, italics, greeks, and flowers in Christoffel Plantin's *Index characterum* of 1567, reproduced in a reprint by Douglas McMurtrie of 1924. He concluded that some of Fell's types were French of the sixteenth century.

By 1925, when the tercentenary of Fell's birth was due for celebration, Morison had won a reputation as the chief British authority on the history of printing type. In that year the Delegates of the Press at Oxford marked their appreciation of Fell's benefaction by issuing a handsome volume of specimen pages set in his types and asked Morison to undertake a 'scientific account' of the subject.

The 'scientific account' occupied Morison at intervals for the rest of his life and was published the day after his death as *John Fell, the University Press, and the 'Fell' Types* [143].

THE

ROMAN   ITALIC

AND BLACK LETTER

GIVEN TO THE UNIVERSITY
CIRCA 1672

BY

Dʳ JOHN FELL

Student of Christ Church 1637–1660
Canon 1660; Dean 1660–1686

VICE-CHANCELLOR OF THE UNIVERSITY
1660

BISHOP OF OXFORD
1675–1686

OXFORD
PRINTED AT THE UNIVERSITY PRESS
1930

140   *Title leaf to broadsheet type specimens 23 × 18 in.*

139. Reproduction of the type specimen of Konrad Berner, Frankfurt, 1592, from 'Type specimen facsimiles. Reproductions of fifteen type specimen sheets issued between the sixteenth and eighteenth centuries'. General editor: John Dreyfus. With an introductory essay by Stanley Morison. Bowes & Bowes; Putnam: London, 1963

This is a reproduction of the collotype, made from the only recorded copy of the Berner specimen sheet, which Gustav Mori published in *Eine Frankfurter Schriftprobe vom Jahre 1592* (1920).

Morison's introduction to the folio of *Type specimen facsimiles*, 1963, is entitled 'On the classification of typographical variants'. He also wrote an introduction to a list of type specimens: W. Turner Berry and A. F. Johnson, *Catalogue of specimens of printing types by English and Scottish printers and founders, 1665–1830*, Oxford University Press, 1935.

140. 'The roman, italic and black letter given to the University c. 1672 by John Fell.' Oxford, printed at the University Press, 1930

The first published results of Morison's researches were five folio broadsheet type specimens preceded by a title page and accompanied by a double sheet of explanatory text, 'The "Fell" types'. They were shown at Messrs Bumpus' premises in London at an exhibition of the Oxford University Press's work, and included all that were then believed to be Fell types, except for the exotics. On the broadside devoted to their history Morison proved that several of the small sizes were cut, not in the seventeenth, but in the sixteenth century, and were of French origin and style. His practised eye distinguished two groups at least among the types, and later study of surviving documents enabled him to refute the attribution to a single Dutch provenance. Other

faces were presently traced to their sixteenth-century Antwerp and Frankfurt sources.

141. 'A specimen of the roman, italic, black-letter, greek, exotic and other typographical material bequeathed to the University of Oxford by John Fell d. 1686.' Printed at the University Press, Oxford, 1933. Proof, with manuscript corrections and additions by Morison

(*Lent by the Printer to the University, Oxford*)

Now that he had proved that many of the Fell types were older by a century than had been previously supposed, Morison began to draft a specimen of the types together with his conclusions on their provenance, as a supplement not only to R. W. Chapman's *Specimens of books printed at Oxford* (1925) but to the pioneer researches of Horace Hart, *Notes on a centenary of typography at the University Press, Oxford, 1693–1794* (1900). Morison explained: 'a portable condensation of Hart was made...and this, with details since gathered together, was set up in 1933. A revise was made in 1936...As copies to the number of half a dozen were printed in 1933 for working purposes and one at least found its way into a bookseller's catalogue, it may be as well to state here that the 1933 production amounted to 22 pages of text in quarto format and was printed as a proof of "work in progress" only.'* Despite the title it contained only roman, italic and greek in a form convenient for further study. Morison's work on the Fell types was not resumed until the Oxford University Printer in 1950 printed an octavo specimen of Fell types as a Printer's keepsake. It contained a revision of Morison's 1930 broadside text and a postscript by Morison.

This is the copy of the 1936 'revise' of the 1933 print to which Morison refers above. John Carter

* Preface, p. vi, *John Fell: The University Press and the 'Fell' types* (1967).

found it in a bookshop and restored it to Morison in 1951. Morison in 1957, in clearing up his Fell papers, sent it back to Carter (who later presented it to the University Printer) with an inscription, in the course of which he recorded that his ink annotations were made in 1953. These annotations together with the specimens themselves ('mostly re-set, as batters had occurred during the several movings of the chase in the intervening twenty-eight years') were the copy for the 1953 *Notes towards a specimen.*

142. **'Notes towards a specimen of the ancient typographical materials principally collected and bequeathed to the University of Oxford by Dr John Fell, d. 1686. I. Types for Latin and the vernacular, blackletter, roman, italic.' Privately printed at the University Press, Oxford, 1953**

A second revise of the 1933 *Specimen* was printed in September 1953, rearranged and amplified; it consisted of roman, italic and black letter. Later in the same year similar fascicules were printed showing specimens of greek and flowers, also compiled by Morison. The specimen for exotics by Harry Carter appeared in 1957. Fifty copies of each were printed for circulation among people likely to be able to supplement or correct the information in them.

143. **'John Fell, the University Press and the "Fell" types. The punches and matrices designed for printing in Greek, Latin, English and oriental languages bequeathed in 1686 to the University of Oxford by John Fell.' By Stanley Morison with the assistance of Harry Carter. Oxford: at the Clarendon Press, 1967**

In 1958 Morison began work on the manuscript of the last of his great folios which was finally published in 1967, on the day after his death, in an edition of 1000 copies printed from Fell types specially cast from the original matrices. The text was composed by hand in the roman and italic of English size and the footnotes in long primer.

Morison's introduction includes a review of learned printing up to Fell's time and a detailed account of Fell's life, opinions and achievement; there are outlines of the evolution both of letter-forms and type ornaments. This comprehensive approach to a technical investigation is what, by then, one might well expect from Morison's ceaseless endeavour to see the connexions between things. It also illustrates his methods of learning and working, to both of which he alludes, in a letter to Harry Carter of 16 July 1957: 'In writing this sort of stuff I have to keep up my interest in the subject by pursuing side issues which, because they are novel enough to me at the time, remain in the typescript because I did not want altogether to forget the point, irrelevant and controversial as it might be.'

In the later stages of the investigation Morison, hampered by bad sight and a variety of business, had to delegate a good deal of research to J. S. G. Simmons and Harry Carter, helped by the staff of the Plantin-Moretus Museum. E. G. W. Bill collected material for a life of Fell. That the book was finished says much for the encouragement and prompting of Charles Batey, then Printer to the University.

Morison was pleased with an advance copy he was sent. He had cleared up nearly all the mystery surrounding the origin of the types and found among them survivors from the great age of letter-cutting in France. He enlarged on their calligraphic antecedents, and provided an account of the life and times of Bishop Fell, spiced with Morison's views on the Anglican religious settlement. The book is a monument to his erudition.

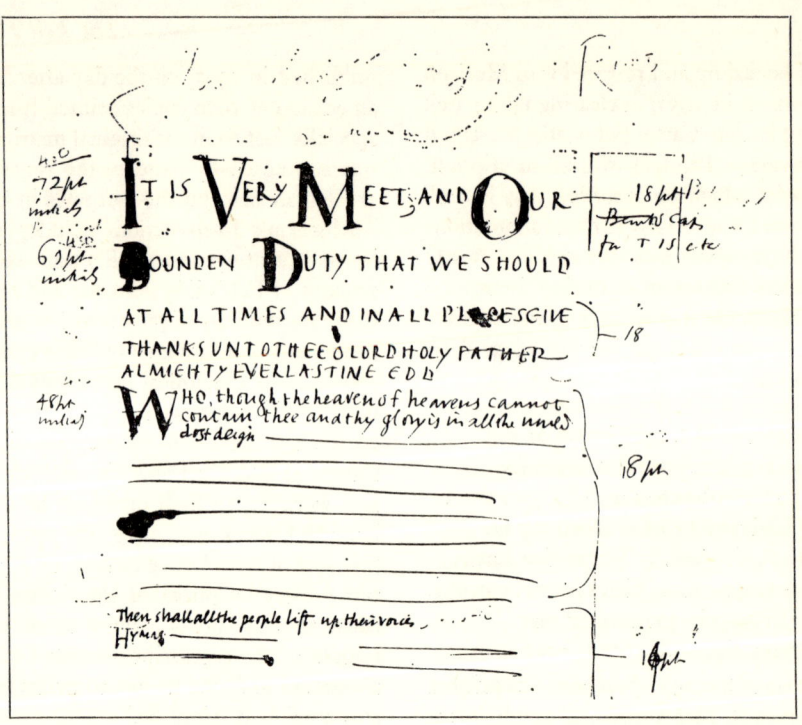

IT IS VERY MEET AND OUR
BOUNDEN DUTY THAT WE SHOULD
AT ALL TIMES AND IN ALL PLACES GIVE
THANKS UNTO THEE O LORD HOLY FATHER
ALMIGHTY EVERLASTINE GDD
WHO, though the heaven of heavens cannot
contain thee and thy glory is in all the world
dost deign

Then shall all the people lift up their voices
Hymn

Then shall the Dean say:

IT IS VERY MEET RIGHT
AND OUR BOUNDEN DUTY
THAT WE SHOULD AT ALL TIMES
AND IN ALL PLACES GIVE THANKS
UNTO THEE O LORD HOLY FATHER
ALMIGHTY EVERLASTING GOD.

WHO, though the heaven of heavens cannot contain thee, and thy glory is in all the world, dost deign to hallow places for thy worship that the majesty of thy glory may be revealed and gifts of grace poured forth upon thy faithful people.

THEREFORE with Angels and Archangels, and with all the Company of Heaven, we laud and magnify thy

146   *Page size* $14\frac{1}{2} \times 10$ in.

144. Specimen pages of 'The Book of Common Prayer according to the use of the Protestant Episcopal Church in the United States of America', 1927. (Printed by the Cambridge University Press)
— Title-page
— 'The Order of Daily Morning Prayer', p. 1
— 'Notes [by Morison] to accompany the specimen pages'
(*Lent by the University Printing House, Cambridge*)
The printing of an edition of the American Book of Common Prayer was estimated for by both the Oxford and Cambridge University Presses, who both prepared specimen pages. The 'Notes' were written to explain the size, leading and full inking of the type (Monotype Baskerville), the rubrication, the use of italics, and the absence of decoration.

The book was eventually printed by Updike at the Merrymount Press, Boston.

145. 'The form and order of the service that is to be performed and the ceremonies to be observed in the Coronation of Their Majesties King George VI & Queen Elizabeth in the Abbey Church of Westminster on Wednesday the 12th day of May 1937.' Cambridge University Press
— Title-page opening
The King's (or Queen's) Printer and the Presses of Oxford and Cambridge Universities, who have licences to print the Authorized Version of the Bible and the Book of Common Prayer, have the right to print orders of service for Coronations. Morison designed the order printed at Cambridge in 1937 in re-cut Bembo. The Royal Arms were designed by Reynolds Stone.

John Dreyfus (*Signature*, March 1947, p. 21) cites this design as an imposing example of the advantages of placing the 'contents' of a book on the page facing the title-page. 'The use of rubrication is both handsome and rational, since it serves to draw the eye to the vital words "Coronation of Their Majesties" before the eye reads the verso page.'

146. Liverpool Cathedral: 'Solemn entrance in time of war', 1942
— Morison's sketch for the layout, p. 13
(*Lent by John Carter Esq.*)
The Dean of Liverpool, Dr F. W. Dwelly, engaged the Cambridge University Press to print a service for the opening in 1941 of the newly completed portions of the nave of the Anglican cathedral. *Solemn entrance in time of war* appeared in two editions of which the 'swagger' demy quarto edition for presentation to King George VI was, as Brooke Crutchley says, 'undoubtedly the most impressive piece of liturgical printing that Morison ever designed'.

Morison's characteristically rough and rapidly drawn sketch for the layout is shown beside the printed page, in which roman capitals are unusually but effectively used.

147. 'English Prayer Books. An introduction to the literature of Christian public worship.' Cambridge, at the University Press, 1943
The Dean of Liverpool was planning a series of books on 'problems of worship' to be published by the Radcliffe Liturgical Library at Liverpool Cathedral, and Morison readily allowed himself to be drawn into the project. Only one book in fact appeared, Morison's own *English Prayer Books*, a short but erudite account of the history and

bibliography of liturgical books in England – not only of the *Book of Common Prayer*. This book was remarkable for the number of words printed per square inch of paper, far ahead of 'war economy standards'.

148. Breviarium romanum. Londini,
     apud Burns, Oates & Washbourne,
     1946   (*Lent by John Carter Esq.*)

About 1941 Burns & Oates approached Morison about the printing of a Roman Breviary: four volumes, each of well over a thousand pages and in double column and two colours, which the Cambridge University Press did not manage to complete till the war was over. The machining, of uneven quality on indifferent papers, was done elsewhere. Morison liked to introduce wood engravings into his books, and the Breviary was embellished by Reynolds Stone's work, for which he always had the highest regard.

Morison was proud of this book, combining as it did his enthusiasms for good printing and for the Catholic liturgy, and produced in the difficult conditions of war-time.

TELEGRAM FORMS

149. Post Office telegram forms, before
     and after redesign by Morison
               (*Lent by the Post Office*)

The Post Office telegram form was re-designed by Morison *c.* 1935. He first convinced the Post Office of the need to reconsider the wording and to reduce it to essentials. The redesigned form was set in various weights and sizes of Gill Sans.

150. Telegram forms of Cable and Wireless
     Ltd, before and after redesign by
     Morison   (*Lent by John Carter Esq.*)

Ivor Fraser of Cable & Wireless Ltd asked Morison to redesign all the company's forms and stationery.

Morison in a letter to John Carter of 12 November 1948 wrote: 'A couple of years ago when you, in your capacity as chairman of the Double Crown Club got the Postmaster General to dinner, I prepared a telegram showing the new forms that had been devised for Cable & Wireless. However, in an access of modesty, I did not, after all, ask them to be delivered to you.'

'PRINTING AND THE MIND OF MAN'

151. 'Printing and the Mind of Man.
     A descriptive catalogue illustrating
     the impact of print on the evolution
     of Western civilization during five
     centuries.' Compiled and edited by
     John Carter & Percy H. Muir. Cassell:
     London, 1967. Title-page engravings
     by Reynolds Stone

152. Photograph of Morison and Harry
     Carter at the exhibition 'Printing and
     the Mind of Man', Earls Court, July
     1963   (*Lent by John Dreyfus Esq.*)

The exhibition *Printing and the Mind of Man* originated in Morison's suggestion that the eleventh International Printing Machinery and Allied Trades Exhibition (IPEX), due to be held in London in July 1963, presented an opportunity of illustrating to the printing industry its own historical evolution and of reminding the general public what civilization owes to print. The Gutenberg Quincentenary exhibition at the Fitzwilliam Museum, Cambridge, 1940, organized by Brooke Crutchley, the Printer to the University of Cambridge, had closed after ten days because of the war. The catalogue (to which Morison had contributed) was nevertheless in great demand as a record of the uses to which movable type had been put, and Morison bore the whole enterprise in mind until the time was ripe for a similar exhibition. The successful attachment of a historical annexe to an industrial exhibition was carried through largely by Morison's personal

authority as a mentor to the printing trade, and by the enthusiasm of his friend Jack Matson of the Monotype Corporation, president of the Association of British Manufacturers of Printers' Machinery.

Morison intended from the first that the exhibition catalogue should be followed by a fuller published exposition of its contents than was possible in the octavo guide. In December 1963 the disbanding Supervisory Committee confirmed the delegation of this task to the joint editors, John Carter and Percy Muir, assisted by the members of the Historical Sub-committee. Three years later the folio *Printing and the Mind of Man* was published in London and New York.

MORISON: THE MAN

HONOURS

153. 'The art of printing'. The Hertz Lecture on Aspects of Art for 1937, delivered on 17 November, in Proceedings of the British Academy, vol. xxiii [1938]

The theory Morison referred to in his annotation on *The craft of printing*, 1921 [20], is set out.

Morison was especially proud when in July 1954 the British Academy elected him a Fellow – 'the one honour', he used to say, 'which money cannot buy and political intrigue cannot procure'.

154. Gold medal of the American Institute of Graphic Arts awarded to Morison, 5 June 1946

155. Gold medal of the Bibliographical Society awarded to Morison, 16 March 1948
(*Lent by the estate of the late Stanley Morison*)

Morison was made a Royal Designer for Industry in 1960, a distinction he had been offered twenty years earlier.

156. Draft statutes of the Association Typographique Internationale, signed by those present at the inaugural meeting of the Association, 1957
(*Lent by Hans Schmoller Esq.*)

In 1957 Morison was asked to become the first honorary president of the Association Typographique Internationale. A record of the eminent book and type designers present at the inaugural meeting survives in this copy of the draft statutes circulated by Hans Schmoller.

CATHOLICISM

157. Anonymous miniature portrait, gouache on vellum, of Sir Thomas More, formerly in Morison's possession
(*Lent by the estate of the late Stanley Morison*)

This miniature representing the martyred and canonized Lord Chancellor of England was guarded into a copy of the octavo edition of More's *Lucubrationes* (1563), which was sold at Sotheby's in 1944. Morison had a life-long devotion to More, and he suggested a sixteenth-century German provenance for the miniature. His interest in every aspect of the iconography of More was expressed in two books, *The portraiture of Thomas More by Hans Holbein and after* (Cambridge, 1958) and *The likeness of Thomas More: an iconographic survey of three centuries* (London, 1963).

158. Westminster Cathedral: services for the week
(Lent by the Administrator of Westminster Cathedral)

This design of Morison's is a minor yet characteristic manifestation of his life-long devotion to the teaching, liturgy and music of his church. At the request of the Administrator, then Mgr Gordon Wheeler, Morison designed the notice 'Westminster Cathedral: services for the week'. Morison in a letter of 27 October 1955 expressed his pleasure that it was to be printed by the Westminster Press, 'known, as it was, to Cardinal Manning, and as it turned out, the press at which I was first introduced to the "art and mystery" of typography'. The block of the Cardinal's arms was originally engraved by Reynolds Stone for the Burns & Oates Breviary, 1946 [148].

159. Photograph of Morison's tombstone
(Lent by John Dreyfus Esq.)

After Morison's death on 11 October 1967 his friends searched for an epitaph. It seemed most fitting to allude to his untiring quest for truth, that urge which caused him so often to bang the table and demand 'I need PROOF'. They remembered the address he gave in 1959 at St Thomas's University, Chatham, New Brunswick, after

the receipt of an honorary degree. The apostle Thomas, he said, was a man after his own heart: he needed to see before he could believe. 'It was not of my choosing that I was born a rationalist, and a rationalist born is a rationalist for life. I see what I see and have seen, less by the eye of faith than by the eye of reason.' This remarkable apologia was crystallized in the three words which Reynolds Stone cut for his monument:

QVIA VIDI
CREDIDI
Because I have seen I have believed

Morison planned his own funeral very carefully. Bernard Dunne of Burns & Oates, for the Solemn Mass of Requiem in Westminster Cathedral on 18 October 1967, prepared an order of service which contained the liturgy both in Latin and in an English translation provided at Morison's request by Prof. H. P. R. Finberg.

RAILWAYS
160. Photograph of Morison in the cab of the LNER Gresley Pacific locomotive '2566 Ladas' *(Lent by Nicolas Barker Esq.)*

When in 1929 the LNER adopted Gill Sans as the letter for all its signs, timetables and other printing, some 90 printing firms under contract to the LNER had to buy matrices. (There was a precedent for patronage on this scale in the adoption in 1917 by Frank Pick, then advertising manager of the London Underground, of a standardized sans-serif for use on the stations, rolling stock, and publicity: Edward Johnston, persuaded by Gerard Meynell, designed the sans-serif letter used to this day by London Transport.)

Morison, through this connexion, was given permission by the LNER to travel on 16 July 1929 from King's Cross to Edinburgh on the footplate of the engine of the 'Flying Scotsman'. This photograph was taken at King's Cross, probably on this occasion.

161. Photograph of Morison, Walter Lewis and 'The Flying Scotsman'
(*Lent by the University Printing House, Cambridge*)
On 24 August 1938 the original Patrick Stirling single No. 1, with passenger carriages of the period, was put into commission again to celebrate the 50th anniversary of 'The Flying Scotsman'. The train, with Morison on board, travelled to Cambridge, where Lewis was waiting. Here they are seen inspecting the locomotive.

PERSONALIA

162. Morison's note-book
(*Lent by the estate of the late Stanley Morison*)
This volume contains notes made by Morison from the 1930s to the 1950s on the history of newspapers, type design, epigraphy and religious history.

163. Scrapbook album of jobbing printing collected by Morison
(*Lent by the National Art Library, Victoria and Albert Museum*)
Morison's album contains pieces of typographical ephemera, printed by himself and others, which he collected between 1921 and 1927, and presented to the Victoria & Albert Museum in 1939.

164. Morison's hat and briefcase
(*Lent by the estate of the late Stanley Morison*)
Morison's black suits, ordered from a clerical outfitter, gave him a studied air of rational austerity. At one stage of his life his wide-brimmed black hat (a headgear adopted by Meynell and Morison in reaction against bowlers and top-hats) had a hole in the crown, so that it could be hung firmly on a hat-peg in a tea-shop or restaurant. Lord Beaverbrook, in his television broadcast on *The History of 'The Times'*, said of Morison: 'He dresses like a Jesuit, always in black, and wears a black clerical hat half a size too small for his head.'

PHOTOGRAPHS AND PORTRAITS

165. Portrait drawing in pencil by William Rothenstein, 1923. (18 in. × 26 in.)
(*Lent by the University Printing House, Cambridge*)
This sketch illustrated an article on Morison in *The Fleuron*, no. 3, 1924, pp. 73–4.

166. Portrait drawing of Beatrice Warde by Eric Gill, January 1929. (10½ in. × 18 in.)
(*Lent by Nicolas Barker Esq.*)

167. Photograph of Morison and Beatrice Warde on board RMS 'Queen Mary', taken in the 1950s
168. Photograph, c. 1939
169. Photograph, c. 1950
(*Lent by the estate of the late Stanley Morison*)
170. Photograph by Janet Stone, 1967
(*Lent by Janet Stone*)

171. Photograph showing (from left to right) John Carter, E. P. Goldschmidt and Morison, taken at Brighton on 25 June 1952 (*Lent by John Carter Esq.*)
Morison was a customer and friend of E. Philip Goldschmidt, the London antiquarian bookseller and author of works on bindings and other bibliographical subjects.

172. Portrait by Robert Lutyens, 1956.
(10 in. by 7 in.) (*Lent by the Garrick Club*)
This sketch, executed in ink and oils on a prepared paper, is related to the full-size portrait commissioned by *The Times* for Printing House Square. At the time it was painted Morison was experimenting with some larger spectacles than he customarily wore either before or after. The Garrick Club, where it normally hangs, was for many years Morison's favourite and most convivial haunt. (Both the painter and the previous owner were fellow-members.)

Tape-recording of Morison speaking about Eric Gill

(*Lent by the British Broadcasting Corporation*)
A tape-recording of Morison speaking about Eric Gill has been made available by the B.B.C. for playing during this exhibition through the good offices of Mr Douglas Cleverdon, who recorded it in June 1961. The recording was the basis of a programme on Morison broadcast in February 1969, a transcript of which was published: Nicolas Barker and Douglas Cleverdon: *Stanley Morison 1889–1967, a radio portrait*. (W. S. Cowell: Ipswich, 1969.)

141

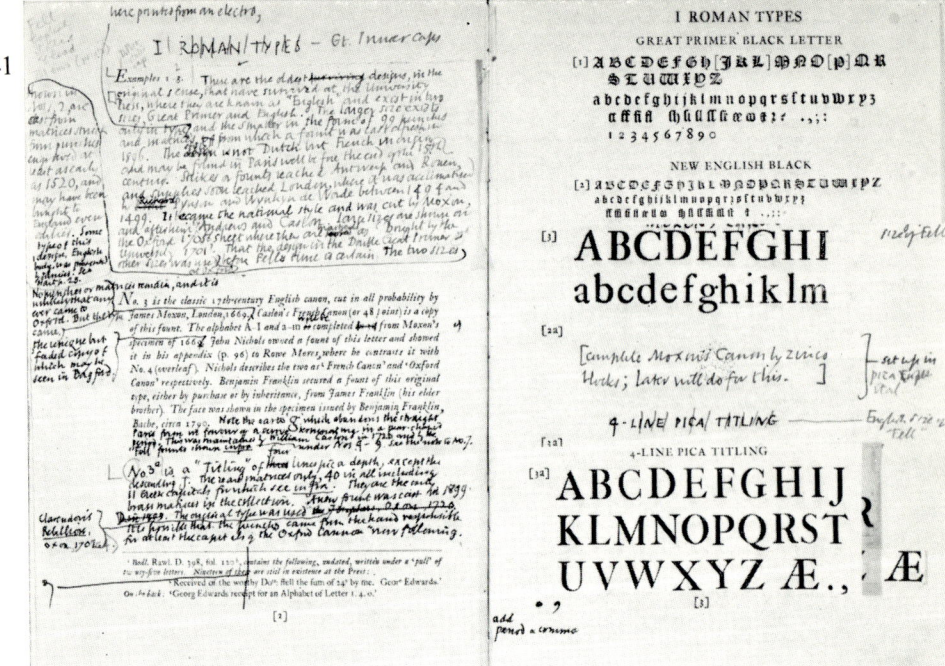

I ROMAN TYPES

GREAT PRIMER BLACK LETTER

[1] ABCDEFGH[JKL]MNO[P]QR STUWIPZ
abcdefghijklmnopqrsstuvwxyz
ſſ ſſ ch ſi ſt ſ ſ ſ œ œ ; : ., ;:
1234567890

NEW ENGLISH BLACK

[2] ABCDEFGHJKL MNOPQRSTUWIPZ
abcdefghijklmnopqrsstuvwxyz
ſſiſſ ch ſi ſſ ſt ſ .,;:

[3] ABCDEFGHI
abcdefghiklm

[2a] [Complete Moxon's Canon by Zinco Works; Later will do for this.]

4-LINE PICA TITLING

[3a] ABCDEFGHIJ
KLMNOPQRST
UVWXYZ Æ., Æ

142

I ROMAN TYPES

Examples 1–2. These are the oldest designs, in the original sense, that have survived at the University Press, where they are known as 'English' and exist in two sizes, Great Primer and English. The larger size exists only in type, here printed from the letters, and the smaller in the form of 29 punches and 72 matrices, from which a fount was cast afresh in 1896. The style is not Dutch but French in origin, and may be found in Paris well before the end of the 15th century. Strikes or founts reached Antwerp and Rouen, and supplies soon reached London, where it was acclimatized by Richard Pynson and Wynkyn de Worde between 1494 and 1499. It became the national style and was cut by Moxon, and after him by Andrews and Caslon. Large sizes are shown on the Oxford 1706 sheets, where they are marked as 'Bought by the University 1693'. That this design in the Double Great Primer and other sizes was used at Oxford before Fell's time is certain. The two sizes shown in Nos. 1, 2, are cast from matrices struck from punches engraved at least as early as 1520, and may have been brought to England even earlier. The Great Primer capitals are disparate: cp. JKL with the rest except P, which might be a stray Dutch sort originally cut for a 'groot augustijn' body. The English is more homogeneous. Note L in both sizes. This, unlike T, is found in Paris in the 15th century but not in London until after 1550. Certain ligatures in both sizes require study. Some type of this design, English body, now lost, was presented by Junius. See Hart, p. 28; also for the remnant of a fount of Long Primer type from which 11 capitals are missing. The lower case is less incomplete. On p. 96 H. shows 11 lines of a Pica from the 1768 specimen, of which a few pounds of type are all that survive; there are no punches or matrices of the Pica.

No. 3 is the classic 17th-century English Canon, cut in all probability by James Moxon, London, 1669. No punches or matrices remain, and it is unlikely that any ever came to Oxford. But the type came. Caslon's French Canon (or 48 point) is a copy of this fount. The alphabet 'A–I' and 'a–m' will be completed from Moxon's Specimen of 1669, the unique but faded copy of which may be seen in Bagford. John Nichols award a fount of this letter and showed it in his appendix (p. 96) to Rowe Mores, where he contrasts it with No. 4 (overleaf). Nichols describes the two as 'French Canon' and 'Oxford Canon' respectively. Benjamin Franklin secured a fount of this 'French Canon', either by purchase or by inheritance,

[6]

I ROMAN TYPES

GREAT PRIMER BLACKLETTER

[1] ABCDEFGH[JKL]MNO[P]QR STUWIPZ
abcdefghijklmnopqrsstuvwxyz
ſſ ſſ ch ſi ſt ſ ſ ſ œ œ ; : ., ;:
1234567890

NEW ENGLISH BLACK

[2] ABCDEFGHJKL MNOPQRSTUWIPZ
abcdefghijklmnopqrsstuvwxyz
ſſiſſ ch ſi ſſ ſt ſ .,;:

MOXON'S CANON ROMAN

[3] ABCDEFGHI
abcdefghiklm

[For K–Z and n–z see Moxon's Specimen of 1669.]

4-LINE PICA TITLING

[3a] ABCDEFGHIJ
KLMNOPQRST
UVWXYZ Æ.,

[7]

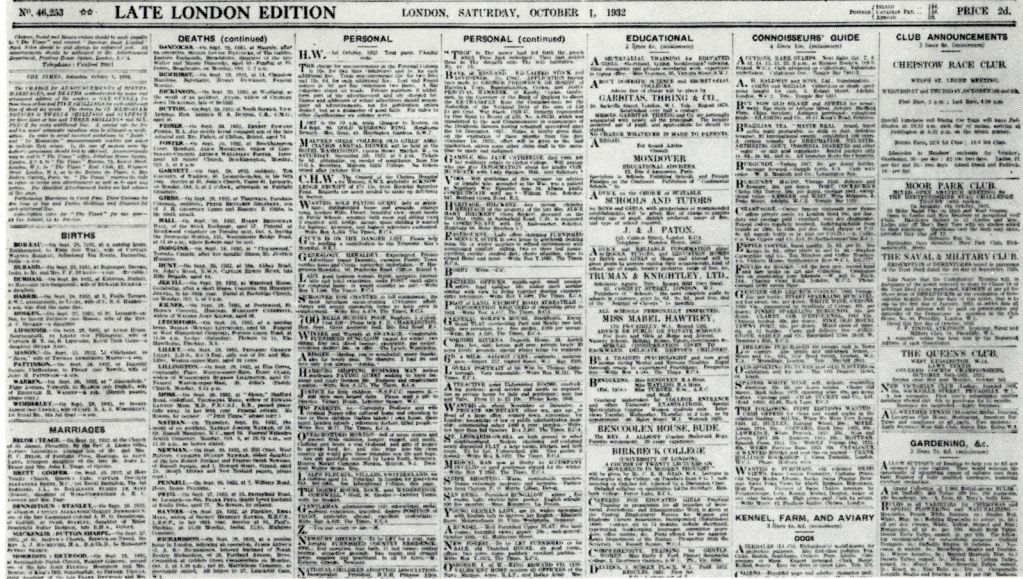

2(c)

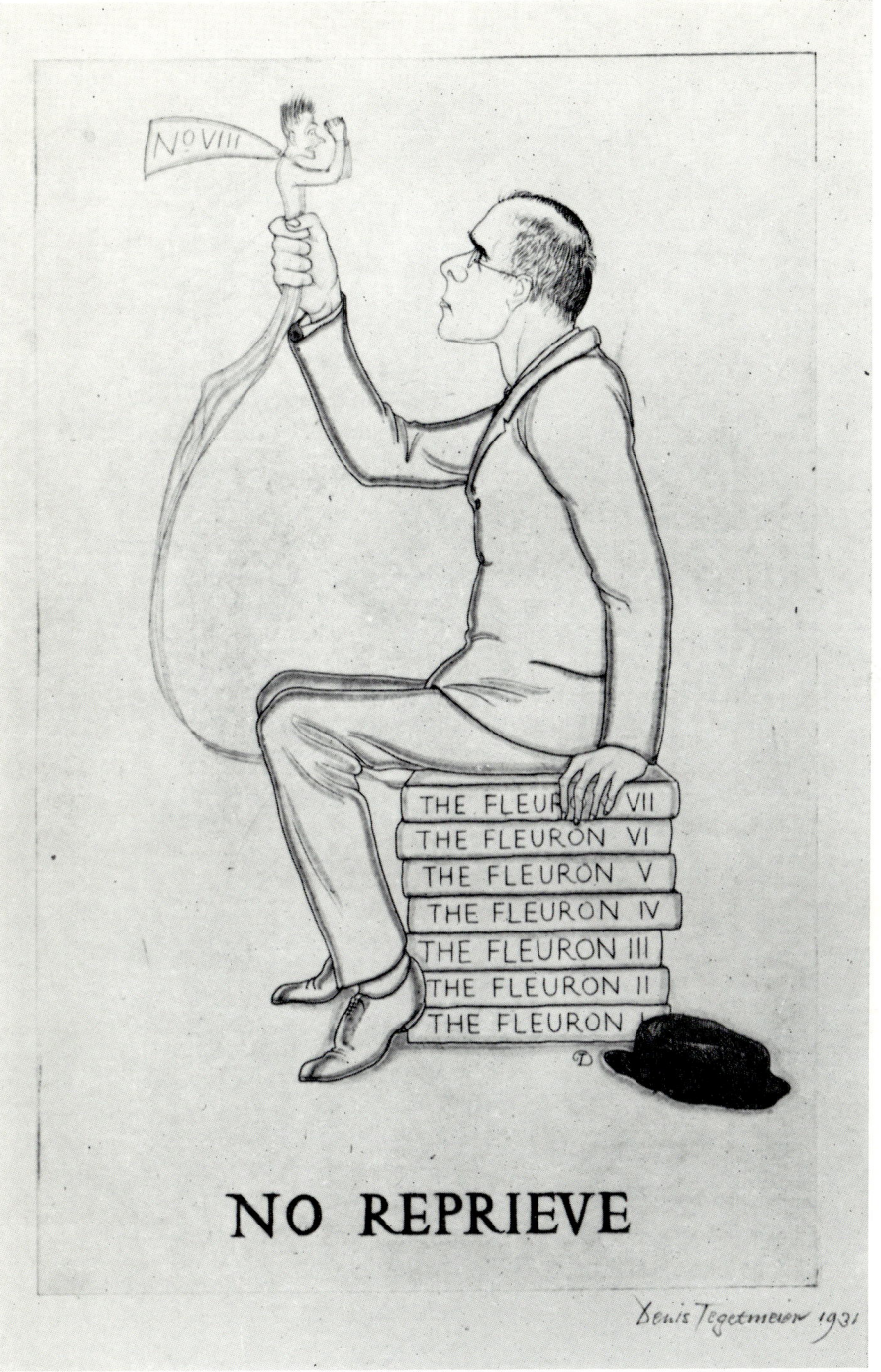

NO REPRIEVE

[$10\frac{1}{2} \times 7\frac{1}{2}$ in.]

Janet Stone

My dear Fr· Thurston
Since your coming
this morning I have
secured a copy of
a 56 pp. pamphlet
THE OLD CATHOLIC
MOVEMENT IN
GREAT BRITAIN:
published (?1918)
by the Theosophial
Book Concern, Krotona,
Hollywood, Los Angeles.

wherein it is made
plain in the words
of ∴ Sis. A.B. that
"it (the Old Catholic
Church) is likely to
become the future
Church of Christ-
endom when He
comes". The
tykes! I will let
you have this item
in a few days as

also some tripe & sawdust called MED-
ITATION for BEGINNERS by J.I W?wood

I should dearly love a few days
off the tomatoes in which to do
a bit of research: I should love
to get one in on the T.S.! I
look to you to smite 'em. S.M
HAMPSTEAD TRINITY SUNDAY 1918-

The Revd Herbert· Thurston· S.J.,
31 Farm Street
London
W₁

The Cloister Press

Heaton Mersey, near *Manchester*

Dear Mr. Caslon: I have seen proofs of Mr. Menut's Garamond and on the whole prefer the American version. For one thing, the original (of the U.S.) l.c. f has a beautiful kern but in the Peignot version there is a f like your Kennerley almost. Would it not be possible to recut some sorts if you had a concordat with Peignot? I very much want to have the cap J (this shd. be a descender as Caslon o.f.) both rom. and ital. cap Q, an original & ampersand for the italic.

I enclose for your interest a proof of the first job in which the American letter has been used. But if I were a typefounder (and I wish I were) I think that as the American Typefounders have a Garamond and Menut has one and Goudy is to cut one for the Lanston American Mono Company I should cut a face which was originated a little after Garamond's time by one of the Le Bé's who succeeded him. It is very like the Garamond in many ways, yet the R is more perfect (both rom. and ital.) Also I prefer Le Bé's M with the trifle-spreading legs in the smaller sizes, the general roundness of the italic as compared with that of Garamond (the original and the copy)

THE
intelligentsia
OF GREAT BRITAIN
BY DMITRI MIRSKY
(ci-devant Prince Mirsky)

including estimates of

Bernard Shaw	Eddington
H. G. Wells	**Jeans**
J. M. Keynes	Cole
G. K. Chesterton	E. M. FORSTER
Bertrand Russell	*Lytton Strachey*
D. H. LAWRENCE	T. S. Eliot
Aldous Huxley	
Virginia Woolf	Dean Inge
WYNDHAM LEWIS	Laski
Middleton Murry	**MALINOWSKY**

&c. &c.

We (the publishers) ask our friends to forgive us: we don't agree with **everything**

~~Prince~~ MIRSKY says. ☞

[8½ × 6 in.]

Dear Mr. Reynolds. This letter is written normally, and therefore quickly, with one of Hazell & Watson's "Esterbrook" pens. As you see I do not practise what so many preach – that all words should be written without taking off the pen.

To my mind handwriting must be 'natural' because it must be fast. I like to see an obviously speedy piece of script. I hate a letter which exhales the scent of some calligraphic cosmetic. Give me a true cursive, let it run as fast as one can make it and at the same time keep it sufficiently regular. If keeping the pen on an uninterrupted line helps let us by all means make it a rule to write so; but it is my experience that it is a restful and an assistance to speed to run on or to take off at will – that will which operates automatically as the result of experience.

This is written 'straight off' on unselected paper

Yours

Stanley Morison

5 April 1932

$[11\frac{1}{4} \times 8\frac{1}{2} \text{ in.}]$

No. 11 Hollyberry Lane, Hampstead
London, N.W.3

Sir: I am preparing a volume on typography which is to consist of some 250 large pages of collotypes & an introduction. In this connection I beg to ask a question of you. I have been interested to notice that your works are invariably executed by the Oxford University Press with a distinction remarkable even for that distinguished office & it has occurred to me that you may have designed the title-pages & perhaps other portions of some of the best volumes. I think the flowers on the title page of Dolben cannot have been arranged in the ordinary course of routine. In an early volume by you (Pickering circa 1870) I think I remember a border of flowers wh. struck me as having been a line-reproduction of the design you also employed for the Yattendon Hymnal. The 1914 Oxford ed. of yr Poetical Wks. has a title composed in a letter wh. does not appear to me to be Fell. These details in the typography of your books interest me exceedingly; may I ask whether you are responsible for the title page & headings to pp. 7, 11, 124 of the Gerard Hopkins tail piece to index of the Spirit of Man? and further whether you would object to any attribution in print.

Asking your pardon for this intrusion upon your time
I am, Sir
　　Yours faithfully,
　　　　　Stanley Morison

　　　　　　October 22

To Dr. Robert Bridges

3·50 · 4·8

[10 × 7½ in.]

East from M

ON BOARD THE
CUNARD
RMS BERENGARIA

31 Jan 1933

Dear Pollard: The Alingan copy of the EBB Sonnets was acquired from Quaritch and it has 47 numbered pages all set much as they might have been if the book were what it purports to be. The sheets appear to me to have been printed dry, not wet as one might have expected from an office in such a time and place. The point taken by itself is inconclusive.

A close examination of the type used for the composition reveals two characteristic sorts which are of some significance in my enquiry.

that prima facie the thing is what it purports to be. This is as far as I can carry the matter at present but I think I have made it plain that an exam from the typographical side might yield something. I may be all wrong but I have not noticed the broken backed f as early as 1850 and if I had been asked I should have said that it was evolved in order to prevent broken kerns occurring on high speed presses, of wh. there cd. have been few in Reading or anywhere else in 1847. This is the invention:

Had you asked me before this enquiry I should have give you a guess that it first appeared during the 90's

There is a l.c. rom f. I have distorted the false kern as indicated but in the original (nh. is printed in about 10 point) it is quite clearly visible.

Secondly the query mark to the fount is not as expected, i.e.

not ? but ?

In other respects the fount is an ordinary slightly condensed modern. Now these two sorts ought to enable a positive identification of the fount to be made, whether S. B & Co Caslon or whose: and it is possible that a local directory giving lists of

trades would also list names of printers, these names may still be traceable in e.g. S B & Co's ledgers. I should hunt up local printing of the time for even if the two sorts appeared in London it would be highly unlikely that Reading would have them at all promptly after their first appearance in town.

On the other hand it may well be that the fount with f & ? was originated in the early 40s. If so I shall be surprised. Secondly I shall be driven to the conclusion

[two leaves each 9 × 7 in.]

126

"A Real TB".

JOHN BELL, 1745-1831

BOOKSELLER, PRINTER, PUBLISHER,
TYPEFOUNDER, JOURNALIST, &c.

Founder or Part-proprietor of
The Morning Post
The World
The Oracle or Bell's New World
Bell's Weekly Messenger
La Belle Assemblée
&c, &c.

Original Proprietor of
The British Library
Bell's *British Letter Foundry*
Bell's *British Theatre*
Bell's *Poets of Great Britain*
Bell's *Edition of Shakespere*

BY
STANLEY MORISON

THE FIRST EDITION CLUB
17 BEDFORD SQUARE
LONDON
W C

128

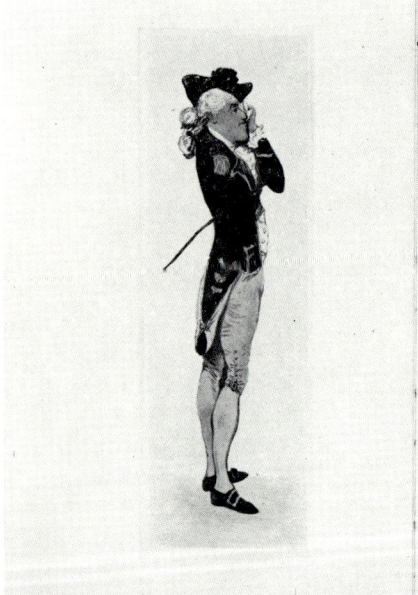

EDWARD TOPHAM
1751–1820
ETON AND TRIN. COLL. CAMB.

Author of
'THE FOOL' AND OTHER FARCES

Conductor of
THE WORLD
AND
FASHIONABLE ADVERTISER

Member of
THE 'KEEP-THE-LINE'-CLUB

And a
GENTLEMAN OF FASHION AND
PUBLIC CHARACTER

Cambridge
Printed by W. LEWIS, M.A., at the University Press
for Friends in the Printing & Publishing Trades
New Year's Day
1933

152

136